Cancel the Filter

Cancel the Filter

Realities of a Psychologist, Podcaster, and Working Mother of Color

Stephanie J. Wong, Ph.D.

Cancel the Filter:
Realities of a Psychologist, Podcaster, and Working Mother of Color

By Stephanie J. Wong, Ph.D.

First Edition
Copyright © 2023 by Stephanie J. Wong, Ph.D.

Published by Color of Success, LLC

All rights reserved. No part of this publication may be reproduced, distributed, or transmitted in any form or by any means, including photocopying, recording, or other electronic or mechanical methods, without the prior written permission of the publisher, except as permitted by U.S. copyright law.

This book is a memoir. It reflects the author's present recollections of experiences over time. Some names and characteristics have been changed, some events have been compressed, and some dialogue has been recreated.

ISBN# 978-1-960299-23-9
Printed in the United States of America

Table of contents

Introduction 1

Cancel the Filter on Me 5

Cancel the Filter on Motherhood 11

Cancel the Filter on Parenting 27

Cancel the Filter on Traveling 82

Cancel the Filter on Coronavirus (in a Cardi B. voice).....94

Cancel the Filter on Being a Psychologist.........................112

Cancel the Filter on Podcasting..129

Cancel the Filter on AAPI Representation 160

My Sanity 169

Love and Canceling the Filter 178

Gratitude 180

Introduction

You Are Not Alone

I feel I should start with a **disclaimer**: **This book is not meant to be an overgeneralization of pregnancy and motherhood, rather it delves into my own experiences and perspectives as a mother, therapist, wife, friend, and female entrepreneur of color. As with anything, please read with an open mind and heart, and be kind.**

If you are like me and the billions of users across social media platforms who scroll through content multiple times a day, you have likely thought, *Wow! What the fuck am I doing with my life?* In fact, this manuscript was buried on my computer even after over a hundred pages were written. Months turned to years, and as I scrolled through social media and saw many of my peers announce the release of their books, the thought continued to haunt me. Because what's more scary than fear of missing out (FOMO)? Fear of vulnerability and being negatively judged. We are human and at our core, we seek belongingness. In a fear-driven world, there is a long history of inclusion and exclusion that is present online and offline. I realized that by hiding behind an image of fear, we are not being vulnerable with others, resulting in lost opportunities to connect with each other.

While there are so many benefits to social media—information is easily accessible, people are able to share their thoughts and opinions, and you can connect with friends, family, and public figures by engaging with their updates, there are also negative side effects to engagement — information is difficult to verify for accuracy, some thoughts and opinions can be hateful or toxic, and that sense of closeness to a person's online presence may not exist if you meet in-person. Many people, including me, post carefully curated photos and content, and teams of social media companies know this. That is why there are options to filter your pictures, such as giving a photo an old school, sepia-vibe, or now with Artificial Intelligence (AI), deleting objects and even people from a photo! Most cell phones allow you to play faux photographer, enabling you to adjust the brightness, saturation, and size of your photo, which may lead to a fixation on posting the perfect photo.

The danger in posting filtered messages, images, and videos on social media is that it may lead users to form misperceptions about a person based on their content, which may differ from how they are in reality. What you see is not necessarily what you get. Social comparison is also based on this filtered version of someone's life and feeds into the narrative that the person is leading a wealthy, personally satisfying lifestyle based on their posts of travel destinations, pets, family, cars, houses, and selfies. I have fallen prey to both–posting filtered content and comparing myself to others' filtered content.

Those closest to me know my schedule: I work 7 days a week (hospital, private practice, and podcasting), take one-hour/week Korean class, raise two daughters, spend time with my husband (at times, 15-20 minutes alone if we both stay awake long enough at night), squeezing in vacations, time with friends and family, exercise, and our two daughters' extra-curricular activities. Based on my social media presence, I often get asked, "How do you do it all? You are Superwoman!" My reply is, "I'm 20 seconds from losing my shit *all* the time." To which they laugh, but no, I am serious... Don't get me wrong, in my 30s, I enjoy a newfound stability that I didn't have in my 20s. I no longer have to compete in Hunger Games-style for the next doctoral internship or residency. I can now afford my bills and still have savings because I am extremely cheap. I have been able to make a life in the Bay Area, and with that lifestyle, comes great responsibility. It makes me reflect, "How did I even get here?"

It is time to move past the curated videos, pictures, and messages by canceling the filter on the realities of being a working mother of color. While academic research is important, there is power in engaging in "real talk" about motherhood, things that you do not hear about, or things mumbled by others in passing. Therapists tend to have varying perspectives on self-disclosure. Some fall into the camp of not telling clients anything about themselves because therapy sessions are not about the therapist, but rather you are a blank slate for the client to make assumptions about. Others believe that clinically relevant disclosure is beneficial to building a therapeutic alliance, demonstrating empathy and understanding for the client's issues, and a sense of humanity. By writing this book, I recognize that while I am not directly disclosing to clients, some will inevitably read it, and as a result, know more about me.

However, my goal is to normalize the experience around the daily struggles in your career, partnership, parenting, and community: You are **not** alone. You are **not** going crazy. At times, you feel that way, but that's okay within the bounds of relatively good mental health and coping skills. I have seen many clients who feel they are the only ones who "just can't handle it [parenthood]." They ask the question, "Why do others seem to have it together, but I don't?" The reality is we all struggle at one time or another because being a working mom is hard in this current society! And, yes, staying at home with your children is still considered working. You just do not get pay, sick leave, vacation time, or breaks.

This book is composed of personal short stories because let's face it, who the hell has time to read a story from front to back while working and raising kids? Not me at least. These stories demonstrate that when you cancel the filter on identity, parenthood, education, marriage, working as a psychotherapist and podcaster, diverse representation, and self-care, we can better relate to each other's struggles and triumphs, further connecting as people. I am ready to cancel the filter on the one that I use most often—fear.

<u>Another disclaimer:</u> This is not a coming-of-age story, but it is about the messy and difficult parts of life and the ways that I have personally dealt with them. Along the way, there have been many mistakes, laughter, tears, joy, and ongoing learning. There has also been a lot of love and connection because of my willingness to have open and transparent conversations with others. I have stepped on some toes at times and have also taken responsibility for the times when I have intentionally or unintentionally hurt someone's feelings. I am not perfect, and there were and are many times that I worry about the "right" thing to say or the "right" way to do something. I have come to embrace my life beyond the filtered version, or the snapshots presented to the world, and I hope readers will also accept the imperfections that most of us experience.

Cancel the Filter on Me

To better understand me, my stories will cancel the filter on some of the common assumptions or misperceptions that have been communicated to me:

- I'm not American
- I was raised in an affluent family
- I'm in my late 20s, which I love hearing by the way
- I am not a mother, or if people acknowledge I have children, in their minds, my children are infants or toddlers
- I'm an early career psychologist

"Where are you from?" This is a common question that has been asked of individuals from under-represented groups.

My smartass reply is "America."

"No, where are you *really* from?" is the follow-up question.

"San Francisco, California, United States of America, but if you are asking where my ancestors immigrated from, then China."

My origin story would not be complete without talking about my family's history, which was revealed to me through an assignment in graduate school. I had to complete a cultural genogram, a family tree accompanied by a narrative of our family's history, norms, and beliefs, and explore how my background influenced my identity and perspective of mental health and treatment. As a starting point to help us gather information, the professor recommended that we ask our eldest relatives to pass down their stories to us. I was fortunate to speak with my mother's eldest sibling who immigrated with my grandmother from China to America.

Stephanie J. Wong

My relative began, "You come from peasants... We've come a long way."

My maternal great-grandmother and grandmother lived in a small, rural village in Toisan, Guangdong, China. My grandmother's primary job was to herd the sheep and stack wood on the side of the house so she could bring it inside to cook. My grandmother was the first woman in her village to not have her feet bound. My great-grandmother was a practical woman, and acknowledged that if my grandmother's feet were bound, this wouldn't be beneficial to her job herding sheep or stacking wood. My grandmother was forced by her mother to marry my grandfather, who was 30 years her senior and a village scholar. His first wife passed and he had three daughters and one adopted son.

The poverty in the village was widespread, and many, including my great-grandfather and grandfather, traveled to America in the hopes of better financial opportunities. Our family history is not unlike many other Chinese-Americans' stories. Dating back to the early 1840s/early 1850s, male Chinese workers were brought to America as cheap laborers, and they came to work *temporarily* with the intention of returning home to their families with their earnings. After all, only merchants were allowed to bring their wives and children. Chinese workers were increasingly attracted to coming to America during the Gold Rush in search of Gam Saan, or the Golden Mountain. Then came the need for laborers on the Transcontinental Railroad, which would enable travel to and from the coasts. Construction began in Omaha, Nebraska (NE) and Sacramento, California with the merging point at Promontory Summit, Utah. Risking their lives to build the tracks on mountainous terrain, Chinese laborers would go on to complete the project eight years ahead of schedule.

My great grandfather (the father of my grandfather) immigrated to the United States (US) in this historical context. He worked on the First Transcontinental Railroad in Omaha, where there was a very small Chinese settlement there. He sent money back home to our family in China, and once he made a satisfactory amount of money, he returned home.

Chinese immigrants were rewarded for their hard work with racial and ethnic discrimination and oppression, communicating the message that the Chinese could provide cheap labor, but we were not American. For example, the Chinese Exclusion Act in the 1880s restricted Chinese laborers from immigrating to the US for ten years. Subsequent laws severely limited or excluded Chinese immigration. It was only until China became an ally to the US during WWII, that the Chinese Exclusion Act was repealed in 1943, allowing for citizenship.

The famine in China in the 1940s led my grandfather to move to Nebraska in search of opportunities. He became a waiter, a common job among Chinese immigrants during that time because they had to provide services to sustain themselves. When it became legal, my grandfather petitioned for my grandmother and my aunt to come to Oakland, California in 1953. They started a laundry business, but it was unsuccessful, and they moved back to Nebraska. Following the birth of my mother and her youngest brother, the family relocated to San Francisco's Chinatown.

My grandmother was unfortunately widowed when my mother was a teenager, and worked over fourteen-hour days as a waitress. She was illiterate and continued to find herself struggling in poverty with four children. My aunt left Chinatown to marry, attend college, and later, graduate school, the only one out of the four siblings to earn a college degree. Like my grandparents, my mother worked as a waitress and cashier. My brother also works in the food service industry, working long hours.

On my father's side, less is known about the actual immigration story, but once in America, my paternal relatives followed suit with other Chinese Americans, and opened up a family-owned grocery store. My grandfather owned the store, and my father eventually owned and sold it. He continues to work as a grocer in a large chain, maintaining his eternal optimism. Both my grandmother and father were born in the US and are considered American citizens.

As a US citizen myself, growing up in San Francisco, California, I attended diverse elementary and middle schools. My friends were from diverse ethnicities, cultures, family structures, and socioeconomic statuses (SES). From them, I have learned that people have so much to offer and learn from each other, and no one is immune from experiencing struggles and problems in their lives. Because I was surrounded by children who had a range of skin tones and there were children who looked like me, I wasn't uniquely aware of my ethnic and cultural identity at that time. While my father provided the sole income up until I was in middle school, working over twelve hours a day, I never felt without.

In our culture and community, there was the expectation that children work hard and get good grades so they could get a stable job, such as a doctor or engineer. There is the belief that academic success leads to professional success, which enables you to own property and financially support a family, a stark contrast to our immigrant relatives' experiences. Similarly, my mother emphasized the importance of achievement and grades in school, carrying around my report card in her purse to show the family that I was doing well academically. Because I excelled in school and wanted to be with my friends in high school, I applied and was accepted to Lowell High School, a magnet school. This school was revered by Asian American families and the student population was approximately 80% Asian American with Chinese students being the largest Asian subgroup. The majority of my classmates in the late 90s/early 2000s worked hard, expected to go to college and secure a high-paying job. Students built networks of friends that helped each other in school and life, which complements Chinese American history of establishing organizations to help members of the community (e.g., raising money to sponsor family members to the US or pooling funds to purchase property).

In addition to my close, studious friends in my support network, I welcomed my high school sweetheart into my life. Since we officially started dating, we have been together for over twenty years! It is the classic tale of a jock meets a nerd, falls in love, goes to the same college, moves so the nerd could go to graduate school, gets married, and starts a family. He is a constant in my life, and our daughters, Ya Ya, nine years old and Oz, eleven years old are flourishing in large part because their father is patient, good-natured, firm, and kind. Of course, our relationship is more complicated than this, and perhaps this is a story better told in another book!

One of the defining moments that led to my interest in working in the mental health field, occurred in high school. Unfortunately, we lost a

Cancel the Filter

student to suicide, and at this time, no mental health resources were available. While there was a sadness that fell over multiple friends' groups, hotlines, a list of mental health providers, or support groups were not offered. Within many of our families, the cultural expectation was that emotions should not be discussed because you don't want to lose face or bring shame upon your family by sharing problems with non-family members. You must maintain your appearance of control, which may present as a lack of emotions, and lead to suffering in silence. It is better to keep your head down and continue doing your work without complaint. Those who challenge the norm by expressing their mental health struggles are considered "crazy," and may be whispered or talked about in a negative light. This moment helped me realize that Asian Americans struggle with mental health issues and would likely benefit from treatment, but the stigma and shame surrounding the topic prevents discussion, exploration of resources, and engagement with services.

Due to this high school experience, I was certain I wanted to work as a therapist, and I majored in Psychology at the University of California, Santa Cruz. Remember, I chose a different career path than my immediate family members and had no clue what was needed to be a therapist. What? You can get a Master's degree? You can get a Ph-what-a? You need how much money to apply? Some schools cover your tuition?

There is so much in life I still don't know, but I know that I am resourceful and determined. I was learning to build my skills to cancel the filter, but I didn't nearly have the confidence that I do now. Given the cultural norm to not speak up or out, I often felt uncomfortable when I would do so. While there are times when I still feel discomfort when speaking out, I learned throughout my journey that advocacy for oneself and others is a powerful tool for change.

I was fortunate that after excelling in a Psychology of Trauma course, a Teaching Assistant (T.A.) and a Ph.D. student in social psychology, validated my promise as a potential graduate student by asking me to join her research lab. Becoming her mentee changed my life. I took comfort in her genuine support and asked, "What do I need to do to get into a doctoral program in clinical psychology?"

My mentor kindly took a piece of binder paper and wrote down courses, labs, and experiences that would set me up for success. I blindly followed that template for over two years. Through her generosity and support, my partner's unconditional love, the kindness from some of my relatives, scholarships, grants, a part-time job, and hard work, I graduated at the top of my major in 2006, and gained admission to a Ph.D. program in clinical psychology in Virginia! My education and experiences, including over ten years of working as a psychologist, have afforded me the privilege of raising a family in the Bay Area, one of the most expensive places in the country to live, and giving my children opportunities that I did not have growing up. We have come a long way...

Cancel the Filter on Motherhood

Remember when I said I'm always 20 seconds from losing my shit all the time? Well, I've learned that's motherhood. So let's cancel the filter on the notion that making the decision to have a child or not is easy, pregnancy makes you feel like you glow, and a birthing plan should go as planned (Spoiler: When your water breaks, it doesn't always gush out like it is shown in the movies)! I have discovered that while you can prepare for pregnancy, giving birth, and balancing career and family, there are hundreds of unknowns throughout the process. Sometimes, the best plan is to be flexible, accept that there will be chaos, and give yourself grace to, ironically, stumble as a hot mess. You don't have to be Superwoman, and I am not even sure how she would handle pregnancy and saving the world simultaneously!

To Have a Baby or to Not Have a Baby? That Was the First Question.

When I was young, I always expressed the desire to have a child, a family. As I went through college, I began to doubt that a woman could advance her career while having children. By busting my ass in undergrad, my husband's help submitting applications, and traveling around the country for interviews, I was fortunate to get into a funded Ph.D. program, immediately following the completion of undergraduate work. This meant my tuition was covered, and I got peanuts for teaching classes, also known as a stipend. I felt lucky because I was waitlisted and was offered a coveted admission! I was following my dream of becoming a clinical psychologist. However, this journey led to further questioning about the realism of having children and being "successful."

The euphoria (cue BTS's Jungkook's "Euphoria") of being accepted quickly wore off as the twelve-to-thirteen-hour days left me with very little energy. It was a grind and I wanted to quit every day. I didn't know how anyone could be a mother in this setting. In my third year, two of the advanced students became pregnant while working on their dissertations. I pondered that same question that people ask me now: How did they do it? I never did ask them.

I vowed to myself that I could not have children *and* be a career woman, and therefore having children was not in my near or distant future, until... My closest friend in graduate school got pregnant. Her plan was to stay an extra year in graduate school, to which I shuddered. I wanted to go back to California as soon as possible, but that wouldn't be possible for another four years. I was tired of the snow, and I missed my friends and family.

When she gave birth, and I saw her navigating the ins and outs of motherhood and education, I began to change my mind. Despite her distress about finding a daycare, working on her research, and teaching, she also gave herself a year buffer to complete the program. I watched in awe how wonderful, gentle, and kind a mother she was to her son. Major bonus: her husband was also incredibly supportive. When I saw their firsthand attempt at balancing work-life, and that parenting could be done *well*, despite the craziness of graduate school demands, my perspective shifted.

* * *

In my fourth year, I had baby fever! This is not an official diagnosis, but parents could identify it in others' eyes—the deep, longing stares when they look at children and the kind interactions they have with them. I had it badly! However, we were still living in Virginia, and there was a high probability that we would be "Going, going, back, back to Cali, Cali!" Knowing what I know now, I am so grateful that I didn't become pregnant at that time because it would've been extremely difficult without our family's help.

Cancel the Filter

* * *

Luckily, in 2010, during my fifth year in my Ph.D. program, my pre-doctoral internship brought us back home to the Bay Area, less than an hour away from family. I became pregnant at the end of the second quarter/early third quarter of the internship, taking me on an unexpected journey! At this point, I *only* disclosed to the training director that I was pregnant.

Pregnancy Was Not a Party (At Least Not for Me)

In my perspective, pregnancy is and was not a party. If I told you, it was the most wonderful experience, I would be selling you straight bullshit. I was completely exhausted during my first trimester. So much so that I was so thankful when a client would reschedule because I could shut the office door, put two chairs together, and take a nap. The exhaustion is beyond feeling winded. It is operating with little to no energy throughout the day.

Internship was filled with didactics and multiple rotations in clinical psychology, which required me to carry a heavy caseload of clients. Also, when you provide services, you have to write case notes in medical charts to document the services rendered. This left very little time for lunch and bathroom breaks. It is difficult to pack and eat balanced, healthy lunches because both take a commitment, and I don't have a "cooking" bone in my body. Trust me, I've tried, and I'm still not interested in cooking. I want to eat tasty food immediately, and I don't want to eat things that taste like shit (AKA my cooking). My husband has always done the cooking and packed my lunch and snacks, which many times included my mother-in-law's food.

Additionally, I had to sit through four-hour, weekly seminars, one of which was reading original works of Sigmund Freud, the famous psychiatrist. It would have been difficult for my non-pregnant self to comprehend the material. It was nearly impossible to focus and understand while pregnant.

A Supervisor's Reaction

Overall, during my first trimester, I struggled to find the energy to perform at my best. Understandably so, I was growing another human in my body! However, when you do not tell certain people, such as supervisors, they make their own inferences about your presentation and work performance.

Case in point, I had a female supervisor who I had already had interesting conversations with—interesting meaning uncomfortable and seemingly mean-spirited. She criticized my wardrobe. She did not think pencil skirts and high heels, nor eyeliner or eyeshadow were appropriate for work at the hospital. I could consider wearing a more billowing midi-skirt, but I was not about to wear therapist loafers—never have, never will. Notably, another trainee often wore above-the-knee jean skirts and never got a talking to. Plus, if anyone knows me, cat-eye makeup is my signature look and has been since college.

Differences in wardrobe opinions aside, this was the context of our relationship. So, when my mentor told me that this supervisor said I seemed to have senioritis, I was very upset. My mentor told me not to tell her or anyone that he told me. That didn't sit well with me. In our next meeting, I came equipped with my ultrasound pictures. I was very anxious. I had already been feeling nauseous and dressing in awful, big clothes even before pregnancy because of her talk with me. I didn't know what to wear because my style had been criticized and so I overcorrected by wearing big clothes.

I presented her with my ultrasound pictures and stated that I was pregnant and that my disclosure was in response to her comment. Her response, "That comment was supposed to be confidential." I immediately feared that she would tell my mentor, but she assured me that she would just emphasize the importance of confidentiality. I had all the confidence in the world that she would do only that. If you didn't already pick up on this, I'm being sarcastic. I just disclosed that I was pregnant even though I didn't want to tell her yet. I felt pressured to give her context as to why I seemed different than I was at the beginning of the training year. Ironically, I later found out that she was pregnant, too, which made me feel even more judged. I also felt extremely vulnerable career-wise, particularly since I needed her glowing recommendation to apply for a subsequent training opportunity. So, I swallowed my pride, trudged on, and did not advocate for myself.

I tell this story to highlight a situation in a training/work environment that was not very supportive of a female trainee becoming pregnant. Many women fear losing their jobs or being viewed as less competent at their jobs after becoming pregnant. At that time, none of my classmates or friends were pregnant, and I felt very alone.

Additionally, after work, I had to walk, or rather waddle with our three dogs in the sweltering heat. My husband was interning with multiple sports teams and often had to work twelve-hour days for two weeks straight if the team was at home. I began to deeply dislike homestands. My new roommate was wide-eyed and right out of college and craved to go out after work (Taco Tuesdays, Happy hours). I just wanted to eat, watch television, and sleep. After all, I had to get up early and push through it all over again.

Birth of "Speedy Betes"

When you are pregnant, there are times when you feel like a human experiment. I cannot even recall how many times I was poked and prodded or asked to submit blood and/or urine. What I do remember is taking the glucose or sugar-level tests. My first one-hour test was high, and I was punished by having to take the three-hour test. This required me to chug a disgusting sugar drink and have my blood tested again. The results were in: I had gestational diabetes, which translated in my mind as: "No pasta or ice cream!" The myth that you can eat whatever you want when you are preggers was shattered.

I tried my best to stick to a low-carb, low-sugar diet from then on out. After the appointment, I had plans to meet my husband for a consolatory lunch at a Korean BBQ spot. As I was driving through the hospital parking lot, a police officer on a bicycle pulled me over. He said I was speeding and called for back-up. A police car arrived, and they asked me to provide my documentation and get out of the car. At this point, I could barely move comfortably so getting out of the car was the last thing on my mind, but I complied. Despite seeing me hobble, and yes, I did play it up a little, I got a ticket for a whopping $65!

After they left, I began to cry. I do not like getting in trouble and on top of being an empath, I had hormones coursing through my body. Also, it was very unnecessary for a police officer on a bicycle to call for back-up on a pregnant woman. Did he seriously think I was going to run away?!

I called my husband who said, "Brush it off and I'll take care of the payment. I'll see you at the restaurant."

When I arrived at the restaurant, and slowly got out of my car, pouting, he put his arm around my shoulder and drew me in for a hug. "Come here, Speedy Betes!"

I clearly married him for his optimism, humor, and high distress tolerance.

**I am not making fun of anyone who has or had diabetes. It fucking sucks! More on that later. I am merely highlighting how partners can support each other during difficult times, particularly with carefully timed humor.

There's a Leak

My husband and I hosted a mixed-gender baby shower with the traditional games of guessing my waist size with yarn and seeing who could chug the most apple juice out of bottles. *Wait, is that traditional?* One of my favorite games was spreading assorted brands of chocolate on diapers, and guests must guess the brand. It looks so realistic! After giving birth, I have since participated in and witnessed new games. One entails two lines of people competing to transfer a blown-up balloon by placing it under their shirt, taking it out, and transferring it to the next person to do the same. This process goes down the line until the last person puts it in their shirt and pops it. So fun!

Well, my fun-filled celebration turned into a week of unpredictabil-

Cancel the Filter

ity. The next day at my residency, I experienced some "leakage." I was not overly concerned, but I called the hospital anyway. The advice nurse recommended that I come into the clinic for an exam. Here was my thought process back then: The closest clinic to work is farther from my house. Therefore, I responded, "I will go in after I eat dinner at home. I have patients to see." I did just that and my husband later drove us to the hospital in the city.

The ER nurse examined me *downtown* as I focused on my packet of study materials for the national licensing exam. The nurse proclaimed that I seemed to be okay, but she wanted to run one more cotton swab. When she returned, she said, "We'll have to admit you tonight because your water has been leaking."

Huh? I thought the water was supposed to gush out like in the movies?! Plus, I was seven weeks earlier than my expected due date. Apparently, I had been having contractions. I just thought it was the baby kicking. *How was I supposed to know?* I had never experienced a contraction.

As the nurse prepared the admission, my husband sputtered, "I haven't read any of the books!"

I slapped his cheek, and said, "Get a hold of yourself, man!"

In addition to my water leakage, the baby was also breached. Due to my contractions and water leakage, the birth could happen that night. The medical team said that the goal was to get from the current thirty-three weeks to thirty-four weeks. The extra week would allow our daughter to receive steroids to facilitate lung development and have a better prognosis. In this uncontrollable situation, I just had to hope that our baby did not want to join the party yet. That night, the contractions came frequently, and oddly, I took comfort in still feeling the contractions, but I was scared shitless.

The hospital stay was highly uncomfortable. Upon admission, I had an IV inserted in my veins. Or rather, the first nurse poked the needle in, missed my vein, and continued to twist it. I yelped, "Get her away from me!"

Pro tips: 1) Always look into a nurse or phlebotomist's eyes to assess their confidence in inserting a needle; 2) If you don't feel comfortable with the first provider, request a more experienced nurse, particularly if you have rolling veins.

It was also difficult for me to sleep because the nurses would take my glucose levels constantly. At one point, I didn't have any more fingers to prick as they were all purple and swollen, so they started repeating the round-robin. They also had to adjust the device that monitored my contractions whenever it fell off, clean my IV, which turned my arm purple for being in there for so long and assist me to the bathroom because of the contraptions that were on me. To ease my discomfort, I looked forward to the sugar-free cookies and chocolate pudding.

Moreover, I still had to study for the licensing exam. We had been trying to contact the state licensing board whenever we could to reschedule but it was now the holiday season and we received no response. In my mind, I had to prepare myself to take the exam a few days after giving birth. I spent countless days reading and listening to materials. Perhaps studying was a distraction technique for the shitshow in which I was participating. However, I continued to white-knuckle it. The board eventually contacted me back, and with a medical note, I was able to reschedule the exam a few weeks after giving birth. I knew it would be challenging to study once the baby was born as well so I continued studying.

I took comfort in my husband sleeping on a recliner next to me every day, attentive medical staff caring for me, and my family and friends visiting or sending their well wishes. I learned that when you are physically and mentally drained, the small comforts are incredibly meaningful. I was thrilled when a friend brought me trashy magazines and shampoo with a pleasant mix of fruit and flowers. I was also happy to see a friend play games with my husband, as he was going through a tough time with me. Some friends even brought movies to watch. I cannot say enough about the power of social support in times of stress *and* in times of joy. I am forever grateful for the support.

Cancel the Filter

<u>To Have a C-Section, or to Not Have a C-Section? That was the Second Question...</u>

Oz was breached, according to the most recent ultrasound, and at one point, she was sleeping horizontally across my belly. Some of the medical doctors said that they could try to invert her so I could give birth vaginally, while others advised against it, saying it was too risky. The decision was ultimately up to me and my husband. We wrestled with the decision for days, up until...

I gave birth. Why was it such a hard decision at the time?

1. We went to a birthing class where you spend hours learning how to breathe when you feel contractions. But not what a contraction feels like.
2. We paid for the class. Of course, I half-jokingly asked for a refund.
3. There was the perceived stigma of not giving birth via v-jay.
4. We were holding out on our final vote—just in case our baby decided to turn headfirst.

Ultimately, we chose to do a planned C-section. My rationale was that I would never forgive myself if anything happened to her while giving birth. After all, when I was walking around the halls before birth, I heard a woman sobbing uncontrollably, saying, "I shouldn't have done it..." I don't even know if "it" was related to labor and delivery, but I took it as a sign and solidified my decision.

Pro tip: DO NOT EVER watch the last installment of the Twilight series. Especially the part when—spoiler alert!—Bella's vampire baby rips open her body to be born before you have a C-section yourself.

<u>B-Day</u>

The thirty-fourth week came, and it was time for surgery. We made it! They rolled me into the operating room for my first surgery ever. I surveyed the bright lights and the sterility and emptiness of the room. The needle was inserted into my spine for the epidural, and they used a vibrator to test if I could feel anything from the waist down. I panicked and yelled out, "I still feel it! I still feel it!" As a result, there was a second dosage administered to my spine.

Meanwhile, my husband was in his scrubs in the adjacent waiting room. He later told me that he was worried because it was taking so long for him to be called into the surgery room. After the second dosage kicked in, it was go time. Thankfully, my husband received the best advice from my friend who changed my mind about having kids, "Stay with Steph when the baby is born and don't go directly to the baby. Don't leave Steph alone. She will remember it and the baby won't." This is a true Pro tip passed down from my friend to my husband, and me to you.

My husband watched intently as the surgery progressed, holding my hand. There was a curtain obscuring our view of the actual surgery. He joked, "Do you want to see? Should I look?"

"I wouldn't. I don't even want to see it," I replied.

Well, if anyone knows my husband, you would have guessed he looked. He looked like he was going to throw up, telling me, "It's so disgusting."

"I told you not to look," I said.

I then felt a tug. Our baby, Oz was delivered faster than it took to administer the epidurals. At first, I didn't hear a cry. But that's because her cry was delayed. The love I felt at that moment is indescribable. I wish I could bottle up that feeling for everyone. All of the struggle was worth it.

My husband cut the umbilical cord. But because of our luck, the nurse did not know how to use a Canon SLR so the moment wasn't captured. The nurse did snap a picture of the placenta—what everyone wants, cue sarcasm—and a family picture of us. You better believe that I was in full make-up because even though my insides were all ripped up, I was not about to look like a hot mess.

Cancel the Filter

Postpartum is Fu*king Hard!

The Neonatal Intensive Care Unit (NICU): Groundhog Day

Unfortunately, when you give birth to a premature or preemie baby, you cannot have your baby by your bedside immediately after giving birth. The baby is whisked away to the neonatal intensive care unit (NICU). That happened to me as well. I was also not allowed to see my baby until way later because I could not feel my legs. The medical team said I could only visit my baby if I could get into a wheelchair. Since I had two doses of the epidural, I could not do so right away, despite my biological, desperate pull to go to her. My brother even lightly knocked on my foot with his fist, and asked, "Can you feel that? Isn't that your foot?" I could not feel anything below my waist.

After many hours, I finally got to see Oz who did not look like babies in the movies. She weighed in at less than five pounds, was shriveled up, and most of her body was hooked up to cords. She was surrounded by other babies in plastic boxes, many born even earlier than Oz. Note to others: It is very tricky to change a baby's diaper and even more so when you have to navigate around cords. Luckily, the nursing staff at the NICU were amazing teachers. My husband and I thankfully didn't have to awkwardly learn how to fold a diaper if it was too big for the baby. We had access to all the supplies we needed—butt wipes and all.

But due to Oz's gestational age, she would not latch. Luckily, I was still able to produce milk, but this required me to pump often. Breastfeeding and pumping are fucking exhausting! You think, *I gave birth, I probably can eat less.* But in reality, you actually need all the calories you can get to produce milk. Also, you have to hydrate with gallons of water. Unfortunately, despite my best efforts, my daughter was not gaining weight. In fact she was losing weight, which is typical for a baby. However, she was small to begin with, and she was being fed through a feeding tube. Therefore, her intake of milk and nutrients was not enough for her to gain weight, and we couldn't take her home until she gained a certain amount of weight. The one silver lining is that she did not develop jaundice, despite a high risk and prediction that she would develop it.

I was then discharged from the hospital, and therefore, could not be with her at all times. My husband and I would go home to eat, shower, and sleep for a few hours. Of course, it wasn't restful sleep even without the baby at home because we were worried about her. A reasonable accommodation would allow parents to stay in a room at the hospital during the baby's NICU stay, but we did what we could. After several days of this cycle, my husband turned to me, "I'm tired of making this drive." We were desperate for Oz to come home.

* * *

There was this one couple in our postpartum class that I remembered. While my husband was pushing me in a wheelchair post-surgery, the wife was hobbling, lightly clutching her wound while her husband chatted with the instructor. When I later shared the pumping room with her, she told me that she had preemie twins and that her incision was infected because she was allergic to the surgical tape placed on her C-section scar. While we were pumping milk in a shared lactation room, her husband knocked on the door, telling her irritably and urgently, that one of the twins was crying out of hunger. It is notable that this woman also washed her equipment after every pump.

I had mixed feelings of guilt and, more so, gratitude for my husband's support. I want to acknowledge that my view of this couple's dynamics may work for them. But I know for me, the distribution of duties is extremely important as well as feeling supported and not alone in this tough situation. My husband helping me bag and label my milk, wash the equipment, feed the baby a bottle, and not leave my side are things I took for granted at that time. Looking back, Oz and I made it through the struggles because of him. Through actions, he communicated to me that he acknowledged the toll pumping was taking on my body.

Pro tip: To partners, family members, friends, and co-workers of women who are pregnant: Contribute as much as you can! It will hopefully be greatly appreciated.

Cancel the Filter

<u>Professional Licensure Test #1</u>

To be deemed a psychologist, all states require you to pass a national licensure exam. Other requirements vary state-to-state. At that time in California, the requirements included 1,500 face-to-face hours with clients after you get your Ph.D., and the hours must be supervised by a licensed psychologist. You also had to pass the national exam, fulfill specific course requirements, such as human sexuality, and pass the California exam.

Given that I gave birth earlier than expected, I asked my doctor for an accommodation letter due to medical necessity, which I now needed to account for pumping milk during the exam. The test center staff promptly emailed me, stating that they would provide me with extra time to complete the exam and that there would be a nursing room to pump milk.

The test was scheduled for two weeks after the C-section, as I would have completed the course of painkillers by that time. I came equipped with my granola bars, water, and pumping equipment and placed them all in my locker with my phone. I was nervous as hell! This is a big day in the life of a future psychologist, and given that I just had a baby, I wanted to prove to myself that I could pass the exam as a mom.

Have you heard of people who are pregnant, running races or actresses pumping milk between takes, and being called Superwoman? Now I was doing something similar, but I didn't feel like it was a Superwoman act. I was just trying to get shit done! Midway through the exam, I paused it, took a bathroom break, and came back with my pumping equipment and a granola bar. I was going to eat and pump simultaneously because well, that's efficiency.

I approached the front desk staff for directions to the nursing room. They looked puzzled. "What nursing room?" one of them responded.

I explained my situation, and he replied, "Oh, we have a break room, and I could lock it."

I shrugged. "Okay."

With no shame, I went to the break room to take care of business because it was either pump in the break room or the bathroom, and I needed to crush this test!

* * *

After weeks of waiting for the results, I had a nightmare that I failed the exam. My husband and I continuously refreshed the test results page. He asked, "What is the passing score again?" I held my breath as I told him.

He let out a heavy sigh of relief, "You passed! You passed!"

The California Licensing Exam

I naively thought that if I passed this exam, it would be the last exam of my life. Well, it has been the last formal test to date. But the true test is when you are practicing independently. That's because all the responsibility of treating patients rests on your shoulders—or license—alone, and not on your supervisor's license.

The California exam was shorter than the national test and I don't recall pumping during the test. What I recall is the printer sounding off as I approached the testing center staff after the test. Simultaneously, up rolls my husband, literally pushing our newborn in a stroller. The staff member looked at the printed paper dismissively, and said, "You passed."

My husband and I then jumped up with excitement. We really did! For those that have been to graduate school, and specifically, if you've become a psychologist, you know the blood, sweat, and tears it takes to earn the right to call yourself a licensed psychologist in the state of California. (Double meaning to come for BTS fans.) I hugged the staff member when he relayed the news, and he responded with an "Oh...kay."

"Thank you!" I yelled as I skipped away.

Cancel the Filter

<u>Round Two: A Different Pregnancy</u>

Almost two years after Oz was born, I took a pregnancy test at the hospital before going to Beyoncé and Jay-Z's On the Run concert. Back in 2013, the internet in the stadium was useless and although I kept refreshing the health app, I could not view my test results. My husband and I resolved to enjoy Queen B's performance and were again impressed with how amazing Jay-Z's voice was. You know true artists when they sound better than on the radio or their recordings!

It was late when we got home, and while laying in bed, we decided to refresh the app, which confirmed that we were pregnant again! Now the fun began, and I asked my husband, "What the fuck are we doing [having another child]? Our lives are already crazy!" Clearly, the reality set in that we were deciding to do it all over again.

Given Oz was premature, the doctor wanted to reduce the risk of our second child being premature. How you may ask? Getting weekly progesterone shots in the butt cheeks, and you alternate cheeks each week. After a certain point when the nurse would ask me which one to inject, I shrugged because I couldn't remember which one was injected last week. I also had to take the one-hour glucose test because I had gestational diabetes when pregnant with Oz, and the results indicated high levels so I was referred for the three-hour test. I fasted and took down the first and second drinks, waiting the respective hour between each drink. I was very close to vomiting after the second hour, and asked the nurse, "What will happen if I throw up?"

"You have to do the test all over again, and eat a whole jelly sandwich," they replied.

I took deep breaths and swallowed down anything that felt like it was coming up my throat. I eventually made it through the third hour. My husband rewarded me with a tocino (Filipino pork) sandwich.

"Give me a bag!" I urged him.

He handed me a plastic bag, and that tocino sandwich was reborn into pork and bread chunks.

The first trimester was characterized by reborn food, as I vomited in my trash can at work more than once. By this time, I was a clinical coordinator and my office wall was shared with a colleague. After a loud vomiting session, I walked into his office and said, "I don't have an eating disorder, I'm pregnant."

"Congratulations!"

"Thanks," I mumbled.

Because I didn't tell him to keep my pregnancy a secret, word quickly spread. He was not aware that most people announced their pregnancy after the first trimester because miscarriages are unfortunately very common. To his credit, when his partner was pregnant in the past, folks did not commonly keep their pregnancies to themselves. I actually had a scare when I was bleeding and I rushed to the local hospital for a check-up. While waiting for the doctor, I prayed, "Please let our child survive and I will love and care for them all our lives."

The doctor's examination revealed that the baby was fine and the doctor noted that slight bleeding commonly occurs when the egg attaches to the uterus. I wish this information was routinely taught because I was freaking out. The fear over the baby's health continued to hang over my husband and my heads. While the vomiting stopped after the first trimester, we went for several check-ups to ensure that my water was not leaking earlier than thirty-seven to thirty-nine weeks. I had already decided to have a planned C-section because I wanted to revise my scar and I did not want to push a human through my v-jay. Although post-surgery recovery is difficult, I knew what to expect.

At thirty-seven weeks, Ya Ya wanted to join the party, earlier than the tail end of the thirty-nine weeks that medical teams identify for the duration of a pregnancy, but still considered full-term. The doctor comes into the room and asks, "Do you want to try a V-back?"

"A V-what?" I asked.

"A vaginal birth," she explained.

"Oh, hell no. I want to do the C-section. I want to revise my scar and that's my birth plan." I insisted.

The doctor agreed and I was prepped for surgery. I felt the familiar pull and Ya Ya was born! Now, we are a family of four!

Cancel the Filter on Parenting

I naively believed that once the girls were close to one year old, things would get easier, but this wasn't the case. A NICU nurse's words continue to resonate with me, "The days are long, and the years are short." While this may seem like a cliché, it embodies the essence of what parenting feels like. To be physically and mentally present with your children is a feat that needs to be faced every day. There were many times when both Oz and Ya Ya were infants that I went to my go-to hiding place in the bathroom, and wanted to assume the fetal position. My hiding place isn't very effective because we don't have boundaries when someone is in the bathroom, and conversations occur. So, I still want to assume the fetal position throughout the week because there always seems to be things to take care of, but I have learned many lessons along the way to not make it a regular occurrence.

Parenting is NOT for the Faint of Heart: On-the-Job Lessons

Let it Go (Cue the widely popular Disney song): Mismatched Socks!

We attended our friend's joint birthday with her one-year-old daughter, which was both Frozen-themed and included a prop campfire (due to the rain). It was fantastic. They had a makeshift tent inside, built with sheets, along with an outdoor umbrella and patio furniture. It was dimly lit and looked more hippie, and "That 70's Show" basement-like.

This was a day that I didn't shower the night before or that morning because of course, I had trouble waking up to go to Korean class on

Saturday. After class, I rushed home to eat lunch, prepare my case notes, and help the kids with Kumon homework before completing four psychotherapy appointments. When I got to the party, my hair felt disgusting, but we made it. The girls were in their Frozen 2 nightgowns, which I swooped up online on sale, and I borrowed an Elsa long-sleeve from my mom. However, we were the only ones who dressed up. No embarrassment, but I went the extra mile and gave them the nightgowns before Christmas.

It was great seeing our friends. Somehow, we got to talking about socks. My friend turned to Ya Ya, "Show them your socks." She peeked her feet out from the seat, and they were mismatched! We then looked at Oz, my husband, and my feet, and we all had mismatched socks! I then proudly said, there are pairs of socks, if you can find two clean ones, you win!

To all the parents who feel guilty or just overwhelmed by the mountains of laundry—dirty or clean—we all feel your pain. Don't be afraid to borrow our method regarding the socks, combining "eaches." There are some things that we must let go of to survive the day-to-day and preserve our sanity. Another suggestion would be to buy all the same kinds of socks, but you may get bored!

More on Laundry

As the kids continue to grow and can now put away their own clothes, I borrowed Jessica Alba's idea from an Architectural Digest tour of her home—another YouTube video. Nowadays, we each have a laundry basket on a shelf above the washer and dryer with our respective name tags attached to the shelf. The kids have ones painted from Hawaii, which were one dollar. If you ever pay twenty times that, that is up to you. Mine is from an office door nameplate and my husband's an MVP award from work.

We all have delineated laundry duties. Dad washes the laundry. I am supposed to fold and distribute the clothes to the baskets, and put my husband's clothes in his drawer. I tend to be the bottleneck because I

Cancel the Filter

can't get a handle on the mountains of clothes. I will say that Jessica's tip helps me when I am folding clothes, *and* it teaches the kids to pitch in by putting their clothes in their drawers. For my youngest, it is always done begrudgingly, but it still teaches responsibility. The bottom line is to get everyone involved in the tasks so there is a distribution of tasks and workload, but don't beat yourself up if the mountains sit there awhile. An alternative would also be to Marie Kondo your wardrobes, sending piles off with a nice farewell, and living a more minimalist lifestyle. But some of us may get bored by the lack of diversity in our outfits, especially those who love fashion like me. Of course, I have the most clothes, and my husband's piles of clothes are quite large because he has spent years accumulating free T-shirts.

NYE Party: Partying as a Parent

It was New Year's Eve 2018, going into 2019, and my friends who have two boys invited us to their NYE party that their friends were hosting in a community room in an apartment complex. Gone were the years, ten-plus years ago when we were obligatorily at a club. This tradition had been replaced with a potluck, and kids and babies everywhere. In fact, all adults present at the party either had a baby or multiple children, and many mothers were taking turns breastfeeding. The mom who was the host was dancing to hits from the 2000s and the current top 100. I similarly danced when my husband played a few K-pop songs, but those were quickly abandoned by others and the mainstream American playlist resumed.

I then watched as the kids raced toy cars, or hit what looked like Bobo the Clown, which my psychologist self knows, promotes more aggression. However, my parental self thought, *Fuck it! It's NY Fucking Eve!* My oldest child was acting uncharacteristically shy and pestered my husband and me to play the children's version of cornhole. I had a sinus headache and craved my PJs and bed. I reluctantly entertained her by shooting the bean bag from "downtown."

Funny enough, we were all struggling to stay awake for the East

Coast New Year's, although we live on the West Coast. We turned on "Dick Clark's New Year's Rockin' Eve" where Ryan Seacrest looked like he was freezing his ass off in the rain. Jenny McCarthy was of course in a plastic bubble (Bubble Girl-Jake Gyllenhaal reference to when he starred in the movie, *Bubble Boy*). There was weirdly no timer on the screen, despite it being ten minutes until New Year's. So, a parent whipped out his phone when the one-minute countdown began. We all joined in ... 10....9...8.... Happy New Year!!

I gave my husband a side-lipped kiss, which was a departure from French kisses or full-on-lip kisses of the past. No sooner than fifteen minutes later, seven-year-old Oz began crying. She was exhausted from the long day. The kids had gone to work with me because we had a potluck. They enjoyed watching YouTube with my close friend while I worked. Oz's cry was our cue to start packing up and to get moving. In contrast to Oz, four-year-old Ya Ya was still jumping from pillow to pillow on a long built-in bench. When we did the magic rock practice from the book, *The Magic*, which instructs you to hold your magical rock and think of the best part of your day, she mentioned the pillows.

When we got home, my husband passed out after putting on a Netflix show. Today was a special night because we all slept in the same bed. Oddly enough, the girls stayed up for two episodes of the show, while I read a magazine. We all then fell asleep in 2019.

Home Haircuts: History Repeats Itself

Finding a barber who specializes in children's haircuts is difficult, and for those that do, the service is pricey. Therefore, I have been giving my daughters haircuts for many years, including giving them bangs, and a bob cut for Oz. Many of my friends and family members who are around my age remember the classic uneven bowl cuts and/or bangs of our youth. My husband and I both have pictures of these haircuts from our childhood. I often tease my mom about making that mistake. I vowed never to give our daughters the haircuts and resulting pictures of these memories.

Cancel the Filter

There is a hack on YouTube Shorts that I have been using for several of these trims. You twist the bangs at the point where you want to cut. It has worked well for us, up until it didn't. One day, I cut at a point that was way too high, and it resulted in eight-year-old Ya Ya having a wave across her upper forehead.

"I don't like it," she said, as tears welled up in her eyes. She then began to cry profusely, but she mustered up the courage to say, "That's okay, Mommy. Don't cry," as she continued to stare at the mirror.

"Can you clip it for now, baby?" I asked weakly.

"Yes," she agreed.

Out of mother's guilt, I suggested, "I'll ask Kenny G (my hairstylist and not the saxophonist) if you could get highlights."

"Really?" she asked, surprisingly. She loves highlights and has several blond ones that my best friend dyed for her. She has been asking for more highlights for months.

I DM'd Kenny G and he said the highlights would cost $350 and up, which led Oz, my husband, and my mom to vote against getting them.

Ya Ya looked down and sullenly mumbled, "I'll pay for it."

My husband reasoned that getting highlights would not fix her bangs. Ya Ya's true concern was that her friends would make fun of her or ask her to take the clip off. My concern was similar, worrying that others would bully her. I did not want to be the cause of my daughter being teased by her peers and having her feelings hurt. I was acutely aware of bullying after watching the K-drama, *The Glory*, which depicted the worst case of bullying I have seen on TV and was based on a true story. The bullies used a curling iron to burn the victim's body parts and followed the main character home. Now, this is an extreme example, but it made me particularly sensitive about the situation.

In the end, we were able to ride out the awkward haircut with clips and gel. They eventually grew out in a chic way, and she felt comfortable letting them hang out.

Stephanie J. Wong

Lies, Lies, and More Lies!

I never imagined becoming a parent meant having to tell seemingly harmless lies. If you think about it, the very essence of creating a magical experience for your children is based on a foundation of lies, or ahem, beliefs. There are countless holidays and magical characters that are accompanied by explanations of lore.

Santa Claus

"How was your Christmas?" a colleague asked.

"Oh, you know, I never knew I'd become a liar," I replied.

She looked at me quizzically, and then I elaborated. First, it starts with—spoiler alert!—Santa Claus. Since we didn't have a chimney at the time, my husband told the kids that Santa comes through the dog door. They then left the milk and cookies along with their wish lists and notes to Santa. When they woke up, the empty cup was still on the counter. My improvisation was, "Santa put the plate in the sink, but must have been in a rush and left his cup."

Six-year-old Ya Ya says, "Santa forgot my Pikmi Pop."

"You don't get everything on the list because you may get presents from others."

My explanations seemed to have satisfied them for the time being.

In 2019, we were working on an extension to our house, and the dog door was no longer accessible. Eight-year-old Oz wondered, "How will Santa get in?" I shrugged. My husband was more focused on them staying asleep while Santa came. He also *had* to mention that Santa came early to the neighbor's house and wrote a note to them, as they were going to be in New York on Christmas Eve and day.

Let's rewind. Santa comes to the elementary school every year and you could take a picture with him for fifteen dollars. Yes, fifteen dollars, and the whole family could take a picture with Santa, as a parent snaps the moment on a cell phone. This picture is then delivered to the classroom! It's the greatest-no-waiting-in-lines-at-the-mall-and-

Cancel the Filter

paying-ridiculous-prices-for-the-pictures. At school, you can also write letters to Santa. Of course, Oz and Ya Ya needed my help spelling so it gave me an excuse to peer over their shoulder at their lists. Oz initially wrote a Poopsie Surprise Doll but crossed it out in favor of Frozen 2 items. Ya Ya was decisive and put a Poopsie Surprise Doll. Notably, Oz got some Frozen 2 items for her birthday so when Christmas came around, she disappointedly said, "Aww, I put Frozen stuff down instead of..."

"Santa probably knows that you want a Poopsie Surprise," I responded.

Sure enough, I was monitoring the prices of the Poopsie Surprise dolls which were $49.99 per doll! If you do not know what this doll is, let me tell you. You make slime with the contents, and you can unzip the dolls' clothes to put the slime in. Then, you zip it back up. Slime is a parents' *dream* by the way. I had my husband also monitor the prices. Eventually, the price dropped to $39.99, and we jumped on it. Needless to say, these dolls were under the tree on Christmas Eve.

The girls left out some soy milk and sour, tree-shaped gummies. Since my husband told them that Santa wrote the neighbors a letter, I left it to him to write the letter. He told them that they had made the "Nice List," or "Good List," and to continue listening to their parents. I added, "Be kind and generous." I was worried that Oz would figure out it was my husband's handwriting, but he wrote with his left hand and in cursive. He doesn't often write on paper, particularly in front of the kids, so we hoped that we would be safe.

Later, my husband was inspired to "capture" Santa on our digital Ring doorbell. We were all already in our matching Santa-themed pajamas, so I told him to stuff a pillow in his shirt. Note that two years ago when we purchased the pajamas, they had sold out of men's mediums so we bought him a women's XL, which looked very slim cut on him. Therefore, the pillow was bursting out of his shirt! He put on his Santa hat and turned it backward because the hat was personalized with his name. He then tucked his head in and went through the front door. Replaying the video, he looked ridiculous! He looked like he was a thief trying to come in the front door! You could tell it was him coming in because of his chin and facial hair. When he tried exiting the front door, you could see the band of his boxers! Let's just say, we did not show them this video.

In the morning, Oz was so excited and woke up Ya Ya, despite her protests. They were screaming about their Poopsie dolls and excitedly read the note from Santa. Ya Ya said, "Phew, I thought I was going to be on the Naughty List!" Well, she is mischievous... A bonus behind the tree was a fourteen-doll LOL Surprise set, which equates to a landfill of plastic wrappers.

We brought the set to open at their aunt's house because of these wrappers, and their cousins had no problems helping them unwrap all the dolls and accessories. One of their cousins said, "I want one of these! I wish I had one of these! Santa didn't bring these kinds of presents to our house! I got a yarn thing."

My husband again butted in, "Yeah, Santa even wrote to them!"

"What? Santa doesn't write to people!" she asserted.

"They wrote to our neighbors, too!" my husband shot back, playfully.

"Maybe Santa only does that in our neighborhood," I said, trying to end the conversation.

Now, my kids seem extremely spoiled, which I agree. However, working with individuals who have been chronically homeless and hearing about their shitty Christmas holidays, I do not mind making my kids' holidays as magical as possible. I will continue to encourage them to be kind and not appear on the Naughty List.

The Tooth Fairy

Now, enter the Tooth Fairy. Oz lost her first tooth when she was six, and I instructed her, "Put it under your pillow, honey, and the Tooth Fairy will visit you. But only if you fall asleep."

Oz put the tooth in a Ziplock bag and placed it under her pillow. She quickly fell asleep and now I was faced with my own questions: *How much money should the "Tooth Fairy" leave? How do I make it special?* My mom told me not to be cheap, so my cheap ass resolved to give her a five-

Cancel the Filter

dollar bill and fold it into an origami heart. So, at 11:00 p.m., I was on YouTube folding a fiver. I ultimately slipped it under the pillow, took the tooth, and hid it.

The next morning, my husband asked Oz, "What did you get? Wow! It's a heart!"

I love this guy because Oz didn't know what I folded the money into, and he explained it to her. She opened the five dollars excitedly.

Later that evening, she arrived home and said, "Mom, my friend said she got twenty dollars for her tooth."

"The Tooth Fairy in her area must be rich," I blurted out.

As more teeth began to fall out, I tried to one-up myself, folding money into different origami shapes. The kids are going to be rich by the time they lose their mouthful of baby teeth. As a result, I'll be broke as a joke because I've set the bar at that level. Also, did I mention that I have *two* children?

* * *

The day after Oz's eighth birthday, we were exhausted. We had a pre-birthday dinner the night before and another dinner on her actual birthday. She had been wiggling her loose tooth at school because she wanted to lose it on her birthday and at school. She put it in the special plastic treasure chest that the dentist had given her and placed it under her pillow. Fast forward to 5 a.m. when she woke up due to the excitement of her birthday party at Chuck E. Cheese, and I had not swapped out the treasure chest for five dollars. Thank goodness, my husband is quick on his feet, and said, "You woke up too early and the tooth fairy hasn't come yet."

I elaborated, "Yeah, Oz, it's still dark outside, and the tooth fairy won't come if you are awake."

She eventually went back to sleep. It worked! I jolted up and ran to my backpack, crumbling five dollars in a fist. I was running on my tiptoes at this point, and the money flew out of my hand. Of course, I did not have my glasses on and was scrambling on the floor looking for them. My mom looked at me quizzically. I gave up and went back to my wallet for another five dollars, hoping that our youngest, Ya Ya would not wake up as I made the swap. I then went into my room to get my glasses, and still could not find the money.

Later that night, my husband scolded Ya Ya for leaving money out and "almost burning down the house" because there was a five-dollar bill on a scented plug-in.

I yelled, "That was me! I was looking for that!"

My husband asked, "Why is your money on the *smell good*?" Then his eyes lit up in recognition of what I had mumbled in the morning about losing money.

All in a day's work, I suppose.

* * *

Oz lost her seventh tooth, finding it in the middle of her bed the following morning. She has always been a wild sleeper and was afraid she almost lost it. Luckily, she did not choke on it! After a happy hour with our neighbors, I was still determined to fold the five dollars into an origami animal. I typed in "bill origami" into my YouTube browser and the first video was of a dinosaur. I was doing well until I got to forming the head. I was not very precise in making clean lines or folds so I decided to free-style it. Unfortunately, this resulted in a tiny, messy ball. I figured this one would be up for interpretation. When she awoke, my husband asked her what she thought it was, and she replied, "A boat?" *B for effort*, I thought.

* * *

Perhaps it's because she was premature, but Oz's six-year-old molars did not come in even at ten years old! As a result, she had spacers and temporary braces and had to get a tooth extracted by the dentist. I felt bad for the kid because she couldn't eat gummy bears or any other sticky sweets she enjoyed. The day before the tooth pull, she asked if she could sleep in her room instead of the couch. The girls were sleeping on the couch during this time because Grandpa was staying over.

"How will the Tooth Fairy know where to find the tooth?" she asked.

Cancel the Filter

"The Tooth Fairy will find it. They are looking for the tooth itself," I lied again.

"Well, Kailey said her dad is the Tooth Fairy," she asserted.

"Well, maybe Kailey's dad *is* the Tooth Fairy," I retorted.

"Maybe," she trailed off.

After a long day, I folded a ten-dollar bill into a candy wrapper, or my interpretation of it, guided by another video on YouTube. I upped the amount because she had to yank out the tooth. Seemed logical! When she woke up, everyone guessed what the origami was this time. The consensus was that it was a frog, despite my comment that it looked like a candy wrapper. Grandpa generously added, "Oh, yeah! I see the outside bows of the wrapper."

Oz moved on, saying, "If I spend it, will they unwrap it at the store?"

"Honey, I think you have to unwrap it before you pay," I laughed.

Pro tip: Always, and I mean always, delete your browsing history and recent videos on YouTube. Oz confirmed that she checks it every time, and I gave myself an imaginary pat on the back to outsmart her for another tooth.

* * *

At eleven years old, my husband thought it was about time to reveal the identity of the Tooth Fairy to Oz. We called her into my office. I then brought one finger over my lips to signal her to be a bit quiet, as Ya Ya was in the other room.

"We are going to tell you who the Tooth Fairy is," I said.

She started laughing hysterically in anticipation.

"It's Daddy and Mommy, but Santa Claus is still real," my husband disclosed.

Oz began rolling around the floor with a high-pitched, "Ah, ah!" Tears were welling up in her eyes.

"What's wrong?" I asked.

She didn't respond so I took a guess. "Is it because you wanted to catch Daddy, and you feel so grown up?"

She nodded, and my husband knew that he had burst her bubble, so he responded, "Just kidding!"

"Daddyyyyy!"

That night, Oz hid her tooth under the pillow she did not rest her head on. My husband was on a treasure hunt for it. This time, we didn't have change for ten dollars and left the whole bill. My husband folded it into an airplane, which we all know he is good at folding.

The next day, Oz accused him of being the Tooth Fairy, but we continued the game of denial, or lying.

* * *

Leprechauns

Another magical being is a leprechaun. Apparently, catching one is a big thing in schools, particularly among younger kids, during St. Patrick's Day. My daughters built a cardboard trap, and my mom gave them pennies to put in the trap. Great, another magical expectation that I must fulfill! How does a leprechaun respond to such a trap? I got a lot of responses from my kids and their friends and teachers.

One kid said, "I got gold coins [candy]."

Another said, "The leprechaun that visited me left a poop on the floor because he was 'bad.'

I consulted with my trusted friend, Pinterest, and found suggestions for letters to write in response to these traps. Some parents even wrote letters on tiny pieces of paper with a red seal! Most letters were verbose. I also did an internet search, and gold coin chocolates were the most common. After five days of conducting research, I said to myself, *F*ck it!* I drew a four-leaf clover on a small piece of paper and wrote:

"Sorry, ladies! Your trap was very clever. Thanks for the gold coins [they left pennies], but here is something you might like instead." I left them each a LOL doll that I had left over from Christmas.

In the end, they were excited. Ya Ya said, "It was a nice leprechaun!"

My oldest, who is more of a detective, said, "It's like Christmas! Mommy, he used our crayons!"

Damn. I hid the broken light green one deep in my wheeled backpack but used the Peppa Pig green crayon to outline the four-leaf clover. I'm a horrible liar so I quickly said, "Wow! What a sneaky leprechaun!" I'm absolutely sure that I averted my gaze downwards, as I caught my husband's smirk from the corner of my eye.

Ya Ya said, "He [leprechaun] draws better four-leaf clovers than me."

They opened the LOL dolls, and they got a duplicate male doll. My oldest decided to paint him and transform him into a leprechaun. She succeeded by painting the hair reddish-brown, green, and his body green and gold. Creativity at its finest.

Oz said, "I really wanted to see a leprechaun."

"We can build a better trap next year," I said.

"Should we set it up again tonight?" asked Oz.

"Leprechauns only come on the eve of St. Patrick's Day," I lied (again).

"How do you know that?" asked Oz.

"I heard that somewhere..." I answered.

The lies continued to come out as word diarrhea.

* * *

In 2020, I *voluntold* my husband that he was responsible for the leprechaun's response because he scowled when I talked about what the nice surprise would be this year. His was a note, written with his left hand that said, "Better luck next year, suckers."

In 2021, he took many of the pennies and left only a few strands of copper wire, claiming it as the leprechaun's hair. What can I say? Our methods are different.

The Children's Formal Education

Like my family, my husband's Vietnamese American family highly value education, especially science and medicine. Both his parents fled Vietnam during the Vietnam War. While my husband's father was a medical doctor in Vietnam, he struggled to resume his work in America.

Only knowing how to read English, and not speak the language, he passed the equivalency test, but had difficulty landing a residency. After almost quitting the profession, he was accepted to a residency in Southern California. He eventually retired as a Board Certified Pediatrician and was awarded an Unsung Hero award for his work with Vietnamese patients who had limited income. His practice was in the Tenderloin, a poverty-stricken district in San Francisco, and he rarely turned anyone away from his office. My husband's mother is one of the smartest, most resourceful people I know, helping to raise her siblings, nieces, nephews, my husband and his brother, and supporting family businesses. For many years, she worked with my father-in-law at his practice and would cook delicious meals daily. While I firmly hold the belief that education is important, the definition of an exceptional education continues to evolve over time.

Preschool

We were fortunate that my mother-in-law was able to care for our children when my husband and I worked during the day. With the recent arrival of Ya Ya, we thought it was time for two-year-old Oz to go to preschool part-time, so as not to exhaust my mother-in-law even more. Our hunt for the "perfect" preschool was on!

In the Bay Area, childcare is extremely hard to come by. The rates are astronomical, and people tend to put their names on waitlists as soon as they discover they are pregnant. Being a new tiger mom, I visited a preschool with a prestigious name attached to it and was impressed with its resources and play areas. After the tour, I sat in a stuffy room with other prospective parents and realized that the part-time program was from 9:00 am to 12:00 p.m., three days/week, which barely covered any hours of work. Plus, you have to factor in drop-offs and pick-ups. Additionally, I almost had a mini-heart attack when I saw the price tag.

I then visited a local daycare center, but the waitlist was long, the classes were overcrowded, and the cleanliness of the toys was questionable. But the care would come at a discounted price, and I knew other

Cancel the Filter

parents who were satisfied with their services. I decided to submit the application and the fifty-dollar fee.

Pro tip: Read the fine print on applications because many application fees are non-refundable, even if you do not get accepted to the school.

My husband and I also visited a co-op, which in principle is a great idea, but logistically for our work schedules was impractical. There was an orientation for prospective parents that included its hours of operation and jobs for the parent. *Hold up! What?! Ok... I could help out once in a while.*

"You must be in the classroom once a week," said the teacher.

Wait, what?! I'm asking for help by paying for daycare and I have a class job at least once a week?!

My hand skyrocketed, "What types of things do the kids learn?"

"Oh, standard stuff like how to hold a pencil?"

Wait, what?! Our daughter already knew how to hold a pencil.

When my husband and I got in the car, we shook our heads in disbelief and disappointment. Needless to say, the hunt continued.

We made another attempt to visit a popular preschool, but there was a year-long waitlist. We saw the very affordable prices and submitted an application because we weren't in dire need to get into the program.

Luckily, the very next day during lunch, we got a call from the school staff, stating, "We are opening a sister branch of the school. Would you like to tour it?"

"Yes!" I exclaimed excitedly.

Something clicked as we walked through the school. This was *it*. The program itself was new but based on the philosophy of the original preschool. The teachers appeared warm and caring. The policies and procedures were reasonable. Then, my heart sank, when I read the handbook that stated, "A child must be potty-trained." We had started potty training, but there were many accidents, which led to my beloved cream couch being drenched in urine during one of Oz's long naps. Also, my mother-in-law's philosophy on potty training is to let the kid run around the house without a diaper or underwear. Therefore, you could imagine all sorts of oopsies, and the care needed to avoid stepping in puddles. If we wanted Oz to get into this preschool, we had to get serious with the potty training. On the way home, we stopped by Kids R Us and bought a Mickey Mouse toilet that faked flushed, cheering when the kid did her thing. We had two and a half weeks. The intensive training began.

Pee Slips

The hard work paid off and Oz was enrolled in preschool, despite her being one month shy of the two years and seven-month age requirement. She went to school three times a week despite it being a difficult transition for her. At drop-off, she cried and cried because she had never been watched by someone other than her family. The most socialization she had received was during storytimes at the library. It ripped my heart out to see her red-faced and with tears streaming down her face as she sobbed.

Thankfully, Oz had a very kind teacher who she took a liking to, particularly since this teacher comforted her in the morning and after nap times. When Oz woke up from nap time, she would often freak out, looking for us before coming to the realization that we weren't there. She often peed on herself as a result. The school rule was that if your child pees on themself three times a week, your child has to stay home and continue potty training for two weeks before returning. My husband, the eternal optimist, said, "Well, she only has to *not* pee once a week because she's only there three times a week."

Each time a child pees during school, you get a Ziplock filled with the drenched clothes and a slip that indicates she had an accident. These became known in our household as a "pee slip." We were lucky that she never got "suspended" and the teachers understood that the peeing was situation specific. The kind teacher often comforted Oz upon her waking up from a nap. But once, she placed Oz on her lap to read her a story, and Oz peed on her! We were mortified. However, at the same time, all we could do was profusely apologize to the teacher and laugh at home. That poor teacher probably went home that night and was like,

Cancel the Filter

So I got peed on today... The next time you have a bad day, hopefully, you didn't get peed on!

A year later, I became close to another mom at the preschool. She told me that her son was also not fully potty trained. Despite telling the teachers, "Yeah, he's potty-trained," her son actually started peeing on the floor during their tour of the school. She quickly recovered with, "Oh, he's never done that before." We had a good laugh!

Defacing Property

When Ya Ya was in preschool, the teacher pulled my husband aside to tell him that Ya Ya wrote her name on a bookshelf and would not admit to it. My husband then approached Ya Ya to ask her, but she scampered away to hide. It was undeniable that she was the one who did it because she was the only student with her name who could write her name. She cried when my husband explained to her that she must tell the truth and take responsibility for her actions. Ya Ya was then tasked to clean the writing off, although I don't know how much of the marker came off.

When Ya Ya got home, I took a more playful perspective, "Ya Ya, don't deface property and if you do, don't write your name on it."

I'm pretty sure that she didn't get my joke. But she never did it again, and it was likely due to my husband being firm. Who knows? On second thought, maybe she has done it again, but listened to me and didn't write her name...

Kindergarten

Eleven Days of Hell

I pray that your child never gets severely sick. During the third week of kindergarten, Ya Ya came down with a fever that crept up on her and reached 104 degrees! It was during a Friday night playdate at our house. We had set up a tent for the kids to play in with their friends. We noticed that Ya Ya was more interested in lying in the tent than playing with her sister and her friends—uncharacteristic behavior. I chalked it up to her being tired from the school week and day. But she became more lethargic as time went on, and began to get warmer, and developed a hacking cough. My husband took her temperature with a ten-plus-year-old thermometer and the reading was over the 100.4-degree threshold. We called Ya Ya's pediatrician and consulted with my father-in-law, also a pediatrician. My father-in-law told us to give her Motrin. Ya Ya started looking slightly better for about four to six hours when the medicine was kicking in. But then her energy would drop, and she would put herself to sleep.

Now if anyone knows Ya Ya, they know that she is always bouncing off the walls, and only stops talking when she is asleep. We liken her to Taz from Looney Toons who is an energetic Tasmanian devil. So, this behavior was worrisome. Plus, she didn't want to eat or drink anything, which led to her not pooping for several days! I was finally able to take her to the pediatrician on Monday. He said her lungs were clear and that he didn't observe any worrisome symptoms. However, if her fever continued, she would have to undergo blood tests and a chest X-ray. I didn't want Ya Ya to have to go through these tests because of my experience with needles. But the healthcare professional in me recognized that it's one of the best tests we have available to figure out what may be going on.

After another few days of the fever, my husband took her to take the blood tests. My heart at this point could no longer handle her pain and screaming. I was told that the first phlebotomist missed her vein, so they had to get someone else to poke her other arm. Ugh! We hoped every day that her fever would miraculously break, and she could return to school, but day after day, it was more of the same. The doctor kept telling us to "ride it out." He wasn't in the office Friday afternoon so come Saturday, my husband took her to see an on-call doctor who couldn't provide conclusive answers based on the results from the blood test. We then emailed and called our pediatrician, desperate to speak with him, and scheduled a phone appointment for the upcoming Monday.

Cancel the Filter

Our doctor ended up being a half hour late to the phone appointment because he was consulting with Infection Control. The specialists wanted to run more blood tests to compare them to last week's results. I "tagged"—a wrestling term for switching places with your partner—my husband in again, but Ya Ya insisted she wanted Mommy. I put my discomfort aside and told her I would make sure she got a good person, a skilled phlebotomist, to take her blood.

When we got to the lab, I checked in for the appointment and whispered to the front desk person, "Who is the best at drawing blood from children?"

"We all do it," said the front desk person.

"I know you all do it, but who is the best?"

"Ireane," she replied reluctantly.

We approached the window and a phlebotomist appeared. "Are you Ireane," I asked.

"No," she replied.

"I would like Irene please."

Ya Ya was mentally prepared for the blood draw although she did not want to do it. Ireane was highly skilled and found the vein immediately, but she couldn't get enough blood.

"We have to do it again," she informed us.

Ya Ya's eyes got wide, "We have to do it again? No!! No!! AHHHHH!"

I began to tear up but hugged her tightly. My heart broke with hers.

The second set of test results and the third checkup did not reveal the cause of the illness. However, the silver lining was that there were no serious illnesses identified and they ruled out leukemia. *What the F? They were considering cancer?* This freaked the shit out of me!

On day ten, she ate her whole dinner and took a poop, and yes, I took a picture of the turd in case I needed to show it to the doctor. We all celebrated these successes, and that same day, she broke her fever. Ya Ya stayed home one more day for safety measures to see if she could remain fever-free without Tylenol or Motrin. By this time, we were all exhausted from worry, hypervigilance, and caretaking while taking turns going to work and helping Oz with homework. Ya Ya would wake up screaming at around 1:00 a.m. when she got super feverish and needed comfort and medicine. She would then crawl into our bed so we could sleep face-to-face all night! Luckily, none of us got severely sick, although I caught a hacking cough. Despite it all, Ya Ya also tried to be considerate by covering her mouth with her sleeve and turning away when she coughed. She also apologized every time she heard my phlegm-filled cough.

After eleven days of hell, Ya Ya returned to school. I was concerned that she had lost the momentum of getting comfortable with a new school grade, and making new friends during her sick time. But she managed. I'm beyond relieved that she was able to fight off the mystery illness. I can't even imagine being a parent to a child struggling with a chronic illness. When you see your kid feeling shitty and there is nothing you can do to make her feel better, your heart breaks repeatedly. These families need social support, love, and help to cope with these difficulties.

A Parent-Teacher Conference to Remember

When Oz was in first grade, I wore my Chanel-inspired dress to work because I knew that I was going to her parent-teacher conference after work. I joked to my mom, "I have to look like a responsible parent."

My mom replied, "You guys *are* responsible parents."

* * *

As my husband and I were walking up to the classroom, I commented, "This makes me more nervous than if I were being evaluated."

We knocked to find that the teacher was still in another parent-teacher conference. It was cold, yet we had no other choice but to wait in anticipation.

Teacher: "Have a seat. So, how's homework going?"

Us: "Fine."

Teacher: "It seems like Oz is struggling to understand math concepts."

Cancel the Filter

My husband and I look at her quizzically. After all, she was one of two students to advance on her math drills the fastest which was forty problems in ninety seconds.

"She has good memorization skills, but in terms of showing her work, or solving equations, some days she's bright and other days, she is confused."

By this time, I begin to feel the tears well up in my eyes. "I don't know why I'm tearing up," I lied. "This is not how I was expecting this to go."

The teacher's voice softened, "Do you want some tissue? These [conferences] can be hard."

A million thoughts were running through my head, such as *I failed as a parent. I did not know my daughter was struggling. Is she even talking about the right kid?*

"She seems to understand her homework when we help her or check it."

"Well, she is probably working on it with other kids, which is good, but she may not fully grasp the concepts. Is she in a math program after school because they [staff at the after school program] don't teach you basic concepts?" she asked.

"No, she is in it for reading," we responded.

"I'm not worried so much about her reading. She is on Level I, and she needs to get to Level J/K by the end of the year. She has issues understanding what she's reading."

I quickly thought to myself, *Yeah, we pay a monthly fee for the program to help her with reading. But if she is on Level I, how is she having these difficulties because you need to answer reading comprehension questions to advance to the next level?*

At this point, I'm bawling, and my husband's jaw was clenched, but he held back from saying much, particularly since I was crying. I already felt awkward, but I was past caring how I looked.

"We will work on it. Now that we know, we will work on it," my husband said. He offered me his sunglasses to cover my puffy eyes.

I went to the car to compose myself as my husband signed Oz out of the afterschool program. It did not matter what I wore because I looked like a hot mess.

We took the family out to eat ramen and after Oz was done, I let her use my phone to read books for her class. We told her if she did not understand her homework, she could save it until she got home. I had focused so much on her completing the work that it didn't dawn on me that she didn't understand it.

When I got home, the psychologist in me assessed her. I had ten chopsticks, which represented ten sticks, and I used rubber bands to represent circles. I asked her to show me eighty-one or seventy-two with the sticks and rubber bands, which she did. I asked her how many tens and ones there were in various two-digit numbers. She told me. I had her solve the sample problem that the teacher wrote on her report card, and she solved it correctly. I was puzzled. The feedback at the conference was not consistent with Oz's demonstrated understanding of the concepts.

Later that night, I was moping, and at one point, I began to tear up. "What's wrong, Mommy?" Oz asked.

"I'm sorry, Oz. If there is something you do not understand about your homework or anything else, ask Mommy and Daddy and we will help you. We are going to work on your math, and you'll read three online books per day through the class application."

Of course, Oz agreed because she is a hard worker. I love my daughter so much. I cried myself to sleep that night, feeling as if I failed her. Here I am making money, working a lot because my career is going well, but my daughter was struggling.

* * *

One strength that I've discovered over the years is being able to write clapback emails, which is a "diss or retort," according to Urban Dictionary. The art of a clapback email is that it's filtered. Yes, it may seem passive-aggressive, but it's veiled in cordiality. Some examples are, "Here are some friendly reminders." "Thank you for your prompt response in advance." You usually send this one if they are taking a long time to respond, such as weeks or months. My email to Oz's teacher was more along the lines of:

Cancel the Filter

Thank you for meeting with us yesterday. Apologies, as I was surprised by the report. Now that I had more time to reflect on the report, I was hoping to touch base with you. I am surprised because Oz seems to understand her homework when we review it or complete it with her, except for this past Thursday's homework. To my understanding, she has advanced on the math fast facts as one of the first two to reach seven. She has not communicated to us that she does not understand the concepts. I felt bad that we had no idea that she was having difficulties, or we could have supported her.

I was wondering how she is assessed on these concepts. I'm hoping to get a better understanding and concrete examples of what she would need to work on. After we met with you, I conducted an assessment, asking her which numbers were the tens and ones spots. I also used chopsticks and rubber bands to ask her to show me numbers with ten sticks. She also read three books yesterday and today and appeared to grasp the comprehension. Could you provide us with examples of what you would like us to work on with her?

I think you mentioned that you wanted her to show her work for math using ten sticks and not her fingers. What would be an example that she is struggling with?

What words or examples, is she having a hard time with—long and short sounds— because I asked her yesterday and she got them correct...?

I also asked her to solve the problem you wrote on her report card, and she said it was not equal. I also asked her to use < or > on problems, and she completed them correctly. Which signs is she having trouble with?

Thank you for the information in advance. I hope to increase communication and collaboration on Oz's education, as we love her very much and want to support her. We appreciate you for supporting her.

Luckily, her response was more constructive, identifying areas of improvement and examples to practice. We were also able to see what she meant regarding Oz's understanding or difficulty understanding certain concepts. However, I was still having difficulty resolving the contrasting information between what I observed Oz doing and what the teacher presented to us. It is parallel to me delivering a poor performance evaluation to an employee with no feedback throughout the year.

Well, we live, and we learn. My husband was Zen-like, stating, "This is not a problem. It will be a problem if we know the problem and don't do anything about it and/or she doesn't improve."

I should have sent him a clap-back email. Just kidding.

Happy Halloween: Inflatable Pikachu

Equally important to academics is socio-emotional development, which includes making strong friendships. To support both Oz and Ya Ya's friendships and connect with their parents as friends, we throw an annual Halloween party. Halloween is a holiday that I loved as a child and disliked as a young adult. In childhood, my brother and I would often draw our masks based on the characters that we liked at the time —imagine Mortal Kombat's Sub-Zero, a character whose power is to shoot ice from his hands. We loved going to our cousin's neighborhood to collect as much candy as we could carry. During the clubbing years of our 20s, I began referring to the day as "Hootchie Halloween," as girls seemingly competed as to who could wear the least amount of clothes in the cold weather.

Now that I'm a mom, it's fun again because the kids love to dress up. In 2019, Ya Ya was dressed up as the anime character, Sailor Moon, and I was thrilled to match her as Sailor Mars. Oz chose an inflatable Pikachu costume. My husband and I got to the school before the parade to help Oz into her costume because you clearly can't wear that all day long. The costume was a hit, and everyone was waving and taking pictures with her. Lap after lap at the parade, Oz was waddling around the yard. After the parade, she was sweating and out of breath. She eventually learned it was very hot in the costume. I do not know how Disney cast members stay in them all day long and now understand why they have handlers.

Cancel the Filter

Later that night, our friends came to the house to eat whatever our friend gets free from work before we went trick-or-treating. Now, before you get judgmental, he worked as an assistant at a company and handles the ordering. He gets the perk of taking food home when no one else wants it. That year, the food included a tray of cupcakes. As trick-or-treaters rolled up to the house, my husband offered the cupcakes to parents and their children, saying, "You want some special brownies?" I face-palmed because this implies that they were weed brownies. Not very kid-friendly! When I nudged him and whispered to him how it might be perceived, he followed up with, "Not like that! They are professionally made!"

After everyone was full, we started our trek around the neighborhood. Oz remained insistent on wearing her costume despite her prior experience at the parade. This time her friends served as her handlers because it was difficult for her to see. She began running out of breath towards the middle of the route but did not want to continue without a costume. So, my mom ended up giving her the pancake costume she was wearing, which was hilarious because my mom was waitressing at the time. The night turned out to be a successful haul. When we got back to the house, the treats trading commenced. As I looked around the living room, I was filled with gratitude that the girls were flourishing socially.

* * *

Mother's Guilt

Despite all the effort I make, I never feel like I can have work and life perfectly balanced. To me, there will always be an uneven distribution of time to your work, kids, marriage, pets, parents, and whatever else you hold near and dear to your heart. I am often exhausted from work. In fact, I feel tapped out pretty regularly. Therefore, on the eve of my daughter's eighth birthday, I turned to my mom late one night and said, "I feel like I'm missing out on some things." This conversation occurred on a Sunday when she took the girls to a friend's birthday party at a jump-house place. The mother of the birthday girl thanked my mom for bringing them because Oz and Ya Ya would not have been able to go otherwise because of my work schedule and that of my husband. That said, I know I am super lucky to have my mom help raise our children. However, although I do enjoy my work, there is a part of me that wants to be with my kids, that feels I should be there. Of course, there is the other reality of chasing kids around in a bouncy house for hours.

My mom turned to me and gently said, "You come home and do homework with them, extra-curricular homework, spend weekend evenings with them..."

"And volunteer," I manage to say, weakly.

My mom reminded me that what counts is that my kids know that I'm there for them and I will continue to be. The act of helping them do their homework, and volunteering to teach art lessons at their school, are my demonstrations of that. Thanks, Mom!

If no one has told you this recently, know that you are not the only one who feels guilty or that you *should* be involved in every one of your child's activities and events. A friend once said, "All we can do is do our best."

Volunteering

I received great wisdom from a co-worker who has older children than mine, which was to volunteer as much as I can. While you typically think volunteering is to be present for your children and to help their classmates and teachers, she stated, "I volunteer every time to drive or chaperone field trips because I get to see who my kids are hanging out with and what they talk about."

P.S. I love my colleague's honesty and applaud Rachel Hollis's honesty about not enjoying volunteer work at her children's schools. My stomach tightened when I read that in her book because working mothers have been programmed to feel guilty for not doing everything, but really, we all need to assess what we like, don't like, and what we have the bandwidth to do.

For me, I stepped up my volunteer game for several reasons—love, mother's guilt, and motivation that was jump-started by my colleague.

Cancel the Filter

    I volunteered for the walk-a-thon, which is where the students ask their caregivers, caregivers' friends, neighbors, and relatives to donate to the school, and the students in turn walk around the school a couple of times. This seemed feasible to me. I ran into one of Oz's friend's fathers and asked him why he wasn't staying for the walk.

    "[Daughter] doesn't want me to stay. In the morning, she tells me to drop her off 'here' instead of walking with her."

    They were seven years old for goodness' sake! I realized that if my kids wanted me to be at their school, I would be. So, I sucked it up and walked around the several blocks for both classes, motivating one of the dawdlers to keep up with the rest of the class. He was huffing and puffing, stating, "I'm so tired."

    I told him, "If you're tired now, you are going to have a rough life." He chuckled.

* * *

The second field trip I attended was to the pumpkin patch with Ya Ya's kindergarten class, and I was responsible for seven kindergarteners. I was hopeful that I would have a seat on the bus, so I did not have to spend an hour in the car driving in morning traffic. Of course, when I arrived at the school, they wanted a copy of my new driver's license. At the time, I was awaiting my new license but the Department of Motor Vehicles did not give me a temporary license. Instead, I had a receipt for purchasing a Real ID. I'm glad the office staff are thorough, but I was irritated by the possibility of not getting on the bus. Luckily, they agreed to wait for my new driver's license if I promised to give them a copy of it upon receipt.

    Each parent had to lug a huge ass bag filled with school lunches, water bottles, hand wipes, sanitizers, and napkins—all essential when you are dealing with kids—but it was huge and heavy! I vowed to myself to make this field trip fun and asked the kids, "What's our team's name?"

    The girls screamed, "Team Sparkle Unicorn!"

    On the bus, I sat next to Ya Ya and her friends. The forty-five-minute drive gave me the time to attempt to score some of my favorite

Korean-pop (K-pop) band's limited-edition merch on my phone, while keeping an eye on Team Sparkle Unicorn. When it was clear that I would not score the limited-edition mug I wanted, I put my phone down and started singing Disney songs with the group.

When we arrived at the pumpkin patch, all the buses were lined up next to each other like a *Fast & Furious* car meet, but Kinder-style. The teachers purchased the passes and gave out instructions for everyone to stay seated. Everyone knows once the teacher is off the bus, all hell breaks loose. It didn't take long before they began hopping out of their seats and volunteers had to keep reminding them to sit down, which was exhausting. When the teacher arrived back on the bus, everyone came to attention. Volunteers were handed cards of all the activities we could do. Luckily, one of the girls' mothers met us at the pumpkin patch so I had some backup.

Once we got off the bus, I asked Team Sparkle Unicorn, "What do you want to do first?"

Pony rides won the vote, so we jogged down to where I thought the entrance was, and it's of course on the other side. I have many strengths, but my spatial abilities are not the greatest. So, although we were first off the bus, we were third in line for the ponies! Not to mention, it smelled like shit, and all the girls were pinching their noses! A couple of them even said that they did not want to ride the ponies anymore, but I insisted we wait "because it's fun."

Some were also hungry for a snack, but I told them, "Let's eat when it doesn't smell like poo poo."

To make matters even more interesting, the person operating the pony ride had a baby on her back and was pushing the metal carousel around that is connected to all the ponies and propels them forward. As a result, I had to lift the kids up onto the ponies. The ponies looked so depressed, and I felt bad for them, having to walk around with kids on their backs all day. Can you imagine carrying a kid on your back and walking around in circles for a whole day's work? This made me regret my decision to have the kids ride the ponies. I did even more when the lady with the baby on her back yelled, "Watch out! It's [the pony] going to pee on you!" I thankfully jumped out of the way right before a yellow rainstorm crashed to the ground. Can you

Cancel the Filter

imagine guiding the kids around for the rest of the day smelling like piss?

Next up, the bathroom break, because of course I had my period, and my pad was already full upon arrival. The other mother in our group helped the kids with the porta-potties, a task I did not want to do, while I dealt with my mess.

Everyone then got a snack as we rushed to the hayride, which was essentially a tractor ride that went in a circle. So, fancy! All the girls were hungry, so we ate at the picnic tables. The bees came out to play, and in between bites, the girls were running and shrieking. I tried to calm them down by telling them that if a bee stings you, it dies, and if you don't threaten the bees, it's okay. Of course, I can't stand to eat around bees either, but they didn't need to know that.

The petting zoo area barely had anything to pet because all the animals were caged. The cutest piglets and bunnies were fenced off and you could only touch them if you stuck your fingers through the gate. We then left to go to the last "attraction," the hay maze. I don't know anyone who went in and didn't come out at the entrance. Previously on the tractor, I overheard parents talking about how last year, a group was stuck in there for thirty minutes! I did not want that to be us. To manage our time, I made an executive decision to call it a day after four attempts to get out of the maze and couched it in, "We have to have time to pick up our pumpkins." But really, I was over it the moment I heard that story on the tractor.

As everyone put their pumpkin down to wait for the class to meet for the group picture, Ya Ya screamed, "Mom! My nose is bleeding!" I turned to see her shirt stained in bright red drops. After giving her small pieces of tissue to plug up her nose, we snapped the group picture and got on the bus. The teacher wondered aloud who would fall asleep first.

"Probably me," I replied.

I fought to keep my eyes open, but Ya Ya and I fell fast asleep. Thank goodness I was on the bus and did not have to drive back.

Despite the possibility of the pony pissing on me, a bee-infested lunch, and the maze that led to nowhere, I am so glad I went to meet Ya Ya's friends and helped her school. It takes strength, energy, and responsibility to do such activities. Not kidding, I was more tired after that trip than a ten-hour workday! It was so worth it though to be a part of my daughter's life in the way that I wanted—to show up. This anecdote will not change Rachel Hollis's mind about field trips though, and of course, it's all good.

Dance Mom

Another volunteer opportunity that I committed to was for seven-year-old Oz and five-year-old Ya Ya's dance performance on Father's Day. I was the first parent volunteer to arrive at the backstage dressing room with my girls. After all, the numerous emails about the performance indicated that the chaperones were to arrive between 12:30 and 12:45 p.m., and dancers, one-hour before the show.

Flashback to a year ago when Oz was performing in her first hip-hop performance at age six. It was our first time going through the performance process. Costumes cost seventy-five dollars on top of the monthly fees, and tickets to the show were twenty-five dollars a person. Let's be clear: This show isn't some rinky-dink performance, but a large production of one-and-a-half-hours worth of ballet, hip-hop, tap dance, jazz-tap dance, and multiple set changes.

Oz went up on stage and lit it up! However, after the finale, it was absolute chaos—parents bum-rushing to the dressing room to congratulate their kids; kids trying to find their parents. It was a free-for-all because chaperones stopped their duties! Oz started panicking and crying profusely, and when I found her, she was sobbing. At first, she did not want to continue dance classes anymore. But as she calmed down, she said she would dance, "Only if Mommy be chaperone." Don't you just love it when the language regresses when their defenses are down?

So, that is how I got suckered into being a chaperone in 2019, in addition to both of my girls performing in the show, and therefore having first dibs on purchasing tickets. This year, we snagged front-row seats, but the cost was my sanity. Ya Ya dedicated her Saturdays to pre-ballet class because she wanted to wear the pretty costume and get a rose

Cancel the Filter

from us like Oz did last year. We told her that she had to earn it. I was nervous for her because she bombed the rehearsals. When the kids crouched down, she stood up. Oz and I also did not realize that their dad forgot Ya Ya's tights until she was performing at the rehearsals.

"Oh my gosh, Mommy, Ya Ya is the only one without pants!" she giggled.

We started cracking up.

Oz nailed her performance at the rehearsal, but I was disappointed that the routine was less intricate than the previous year. Please note that I watch way too many K-Pop/Bangtan Sonyeondan (BTS) dance videos, and my standards are unrealistic. Again, the costume choice, which was also brought up by another mother, consisted of a long jersey with checkered shoulders; tight-fitted, black pants; a silver ponytail holder; and white shoes, which were not included. Personally, I could see why Ya Ya made her class choice, but out of all the dance mediums to choose from at the school, I love hip-hop above any other.

My expectations for being a chaperone consisted of supervising the kids in a specific area backstage followed by the production staff calling the girls to line up for their routine. I was a quarter correct. I was assigned to both mini hip-hop classes because the other chaperone did not show up. If a child was in more than one performance, I was responsible for making sure she got changed and lined up with her group, while watching the other children in my group. The girls also had to wear makeup, which is inconsistent with my belief that kids should not wear makeup because adults shouldn't make them grow up quickly. I made it clear to Ya Ya and Oz that they were only wearing it because it was required for the performance. I acknowledge I'm a hypocrite because I love makeup. However, I did not start wearing it until high school, and it was mostly foundation to cover my acne. For the girls' mothers who did not know how to apply makeup, I helped.

Have you ever tried applying mascara on little girls? It is a fu*king nightmare. I rarely wear mascara because I do not like the heaviness of my real lashes, and you cannot tell I am wearing it because of my signature cat eye. It is hard for anyone, especially a child, to look down and up with the brush, particularly since it tickles. The kids also wanted to see how the mascara looked just after the first coat. Two of the parents innocently thought there would be assistance with makeup backstage and were not equipped with their own makeup. One girl did not even have any of the required makeup applied. Another did not bring mascara, but luckily, I brought one. I handed it to her mother who handed it right back to me and said, "She wants you to do it because I don't know how to do the makeup." So, now I had to put mascara on someone else's daughter, and I did not bring makeup remover. Luckily, her eyelashes were long, and I opted for two coats instead of three to reduce the chance of error.

Overall, the parents of kids in Oz's class were sweet and two parents gave me their phone numbers in case I needed them. One asked how long the performance would be and if they could leave immediately after her daughter performed. I told her that the kids had to stay until the finale. Despite this mom having a party at her house, she followed the rules and stayed until the end of the finale. I am not saying my daughter was an angel during all of this, but after spending time with these other kids, I felt a rush of gratitude for my kids.

The girls in the other group of mini hip-hop were all over the place. One stood mute once her friend's mother took her daughter to sit in the audience with her. Another girl followed her friend around like a puppy dog. She was polite and asked if they could watch the monitors that were streaming the performances. Instead of trying to contain them, I told them they should come back in fifteen minutes, and they complied.

Initially, I liked one of the girls because she helped me remember her name by associating it with one of the former presidents. However, she turned out to have sneaky behavior, and with that charm came mischief. She was often trying to leave to get water. While I am sure she was thirsty, she did not ask for permission to sit at the monitors or to go find her parents, despite me telling her the rules. I watched her while she played hand games with LOL dolls. Then after a while, she joined one of her friends. But she hid behind the curtains or in the corner to exchange snacks, a rule violation because you cannot eat food backstage. I do not care too much for this rule because I was hangry myself. I also think it was a ploy to get caregivers to purchase snacks from the dance studio. I did not emphasize the rules for a good thirty minutes, but then

Cancel the Filter

her friend exclaimed to one of the other girls, "Can you stop staring at us?"

I couldn't keep it in anymore. "You clearly have food in your pockets. I don't care, but you think you're being slick," I said.

They froze but still tried to slyly slip food from one hand to the other's hand. They then ran to the corner, not saying a word. I scowled. *That shit is addict behavior.* It is hard to turn the psychologist off.

Even parents who were not chaperones did not follow the rules. I must admit, I did not last year either. One of the rules is to not take your kid to sit in the audience after their performance. You're supposed to instead encourage them to return to the dressing room to wait for the finale. When a parent took their kid to sit with them, it put chaperones in an awkward position because would you then deny a parent access to their child? You can tell them the rules, which they already know, but I am also not security.

* * *

Thank goodness, Oz's group lined up effortlessly. Oz's group had only a total of four girls, and we met the boys in the hallway. Another chaperone had to watch the remaining girls backstage in my group, in addition to her groups.

While I monitored the line, I met the "characters." One boy had been busy all day with a total of three dances. I secretly thanked the Buddha that he was a boy, and I wasn't responsible for the multiple costume changes. He liked my Blackpink shirt, and we had a brief, enjoyable conversation about his bias, or favorite member, followed by my description of the recent concert we had attended. Then there were the two boys who were playfully messing around with each other while in line. As we made our way to the side of the backstage, older dancers were running on and off the stage to change their clothes. It was more like shedding layers. One of the older female dancers left her sleeves on this large pipe, directing the kids not to touch it.

"Is that her bra?" Character One asked aloud in wonderment to Character Two.

"No. That is not a bra," I said.

Character Two then proceeded to smell it to which I said, exasperated, "It's not a bra. Stop being a pervert!"

The kids then finally rushed on stage and lit the stage up!

The first act was fast-paced. So much so that by the time I helped two other moms get one of my members changed, I had to run back to where everyone lined up. But I didn't see Ya Ya's group! I rushed through the backstage door and barely made it to the spot to meet her before she went onstage. She did so well and took our advice to look at the teacher while she danced. However, when she looked over at our family, she had difficulty focusing on the routine. After Ya Ya's dance, I rushed back to help my other group line up.

The intermission and second act moved so... slowly. Another mom said, "This is the longest hour of my life. I need a drink after this." I nodded in agreement, particularly since I was hangry.

Finally, the lineup for the finale occurred, and Characters One and Two were squishing everyone in Oz's group by pushing their shoulders against other kids, causing them to bump into each other.

"Keep it together, guys, for five more minutes," I said. I wondered whether I was telling them or myself.

As the kids took their final bows, the groups started disbanding and chaos began to settle in. It was time to strategize how to get my group off the stage. The director took charge, and my group assumed the role of the orderly bunch who waited to be called before going back to the dressing rooms.

After the show, I was so ready to leave, but Ya Ya was upset. Apparently, one of the assistants had taken her necklace because jewelry was not allowed. That was partly my fault for not telling her to take it off that morning. I thought a pair of pink ballerina slippers on a necklace matched well with her outfit and the occasion. Whoops! There I go being a hypocrite again... Unfortunately, Ya Ya couldn't locate the assistant who took her necklace, and to a five year old, it seemed that she wouldn't get her necklace back. The director soothed her as she searched for the assistant. The necklace was finally located and returned.

As we met our family outside, I began chewing on the chocolate cigar they were giving out for Father's Day. Although it was shitty quality chocolate, I needed to ease my hunger pains and cope with my stress. I sighed. "You guys don't even know what happens backstage…"

Life Lessons about Money, Money, Money

Along with formal education, we also have a responsibility to teach our children life lessons. One of the most important aspects of life is financial literacy but it is rarely taught in school. Many people struggle with money management even in adulthood.

What is your relationship with money? How much does it mean to you? To me, money is not solely a currency. In this capitalistic society, there are clear demarcations of the haves and the have nots, where there are some individuals and families who go without food and others who own private islands. My consciousness about money began when my father taught me how to count change, a practical skill that he used every day as a grocer. I would bring out my Sanrio box filled to the brim with coins, and initially, he would count the coins with me to form an amount. As time progressed, he would pose an amount. "Make $1.25 or make $1.50 with nickels and dimes only."

As a teenage girl, I was in awe that one of my best friends would receive her $100 monthly allowance from her grandmother. By college, I was on full financial aid and scholarships, and worked a part-time job to ensure that I could afford one semester to the next, resulting in anxiety about money.

The anxiety about money was further reinforced in graduate school where I was paid approximately $12,000 to be a teaching assistant. However, I felt *fortunate* because the tuition was covered by the university and my husband worked a full-time job to support our living expenses. As I transitioned through various phases of my training and employment, this anxiety has never gone away. But I have taken the initiative to educate myself about finances through trial and error, podcasts, books, research, and discussions with others, which has helped me cope with these feelings. I have always been good at squirreling away money, spending frugally, and saving as much as I could. But I knew nothing about compounded interest, tax deductions, investments, index funds, and Roth IRAs. Despite feeling empowered to have acquired financial and social capital—no pun intended—most of the time, I operate like I did when I was a broke-as-a-joke college student, choosing to buy an item at the lowest price, opting out of buying a brand name, and feeling guilty for making any large purchases because that money could have been placed in savings or investments instead. I am determined to equip our children with this knowledge.

The Dollhouse

Oz and Ya Ya fortunately receive money from friends and family for birthdays, holidays, and celebrations. I allocate some to deposit in their bank accounts and some for spending. Of course, by the time they were five and six years of age, they consumed tons of streaming ads for the LOL Surprise Winter Chalet, a deluxe dollhouse. For the parents who have not had the pleasure of interacting with LOL Surprise Dolls, you are in for a treat. Not really. The doll comes in a large plastic ball with an initial three layers of plastic wrapping. When you finally get to open the plastic ball, there are ten-plus small plastic items wrapped in tissue paper. I see the appeal from a child's perspective: the surprise and unwrapping are where the fun is! From an adult's perspective, *I just spent fifteen to twenty dollars to step on tiny plastic baby bottles and sunglasses and add all of this plastic to the landfill.* You can imagine their ask, which included them showing me the commercial several times and promising to split the cost with us. In hindsight, I'm impressed by their sales tactics.

 The thing about me is that I am a sucker when it comes to my children. I know it. They know it. My husband knows it. That's why they beg me incessantly to buy something at Target, and sometimes, I do the "Go ask your father" because I know he will say, "No." So, I knew I was going to cave, but I was not going to let them off the hook that easily, especially not for a $200 dollhouse!

 "Girls, I'm considering what you asked about buying the LOL

Cancel the Filter

Surprise Doll House, but you will have to learn about money and finances first," I said to my then five- and seven-year-old children.

"Okay!" they said, enthusiastically.

I peered down at my scribbled-down notes.

"There are five things to think about when it comes to money—income, bills, savings, investments, and luxuries. Income is how much money you make from jobs and gifts. Once you have money, you want to pay your bills so you can have water, electricity, food, and a house. Then you put some in your savings so when you retire, or don't work anymore, you have money to live. This could also be used if you need extra money if something comes up. Investments are when you put money somewhere in hopes of making more money."

Their eyes were glazing over, but I continued. "After you have taken care of bills, savings, and retirement, whatever is leftover could be spent on luxuries, things you want but do not necessarily need. So, once you make income, what do you do?"

"Pay your bills, save, and invest," I prompted.

"What can you do with the leftovers?" I asked.

"Buy luxuries!" they said in unison.

Later, the dollhouse was in their room with random plastic heads and bodies of LOL dolls because they detach easily. While I recognize that this financial seminar was extra, it will hopefully provide them with a level of consciousness about finances for the benefit of their future. The house was eventually given away for free during the pandemic!

The $65 Incident

My mom and Ya Ya came in with a box that previously housed Ya Ya's garbage and miscellaneous completed schoolwork that she no longer needed.

"Ya Ya almost threw away her wallet with sixty-five dollars in it," my mom stated, matter-of-factly.

In a rare moment, feelings of anger were boiling like a pot of water, and I felt the heat rise in me. I took quick strides to her room and told her to bring me a handful of LOL Surprise Dolls. I began sternly counting, "ten, twenty, thirty...," my tone rising in volume as each ten passed, until I reached a value of sixty-five dollars worth of dolls. She began crying profusely and eventually went to hide in the closet and then behind her bed.

Am I raising my children to be entitled and so careless as to throw sixty-five dollars away?

"Mommy and Daddy work so hard and give you everything. We just want you to be responsible—clean your room, turn off the light to save electricity" I said to both seven-year-old Ya Ya and eight-year-old Oz. Oz understood but then again, she is older than Ya Ya. Oz began organizing the toys around the room, putting dolls in the dollhouse. I asked Ya Ya to come out from behind her bed, and at first, she was hesitant. I hugged her tightly. "I love you and I'm sorry for scaring you. Mommy never screams, and I know that it scared you," I apologized. I felt so guilty to have lost it.

"You're right, I don't deserve this," Ya Ya said, as she handed me her wallet.

"That's not what I meant," I said gently.

She pushed the wallet toward me again, repeating, "I don't deserve this."

"I'll tell you what. I'll keep this for you and put it in the bank," I told her. "Could you help, Oz, clean the room?"

I'll chalk it up to her being upset and still calming her body, but she barely picked up anything, as Oz and I cleaned the room. She had a wounded look on her face, which made me feel worse. Typically, my husband unfairly assumes the role of disciplinarian so displaying that level of frustration was surprising, and everyone knew that she had pushed past an unspoken limit.

Ya Ya bounced back, but it still led me to reflect on my reaction. I realized I was living by these false proprietary rules of hustling, making money, and working whenever I can to give them a good life—my idea of a good life. I perceived that Ya Ya was not respecting me, but what she needed was help organizing her room, so she did not lose things or accidentally throw something important away. At the end of the day, I had to exercise self-compassion. *I am human and it is okay to express frustra-*

tion. I love my kids and I am learning with them how to continue to grow as people.

The Guinea Pig(s)

I heard the question that every parent dreams of, "Mommy, can we get a guinea pig?"

Hell no. I don't want a rat, I thought but paused before responding.

"Why don't you research about guinea pigs and make a presentation about it?"

"Then can I get a guinea pig?" Eight-year-old Ya Ya asked.

"Daddy and I will consider it," I said, shocked that those words even came out of my mouth.

"We will give you questions, and you will have to answer them in your presentation," my husband said.

My husband was notably excited and explained to me, "I don't want to say no to her like my parents just because I don't want something. I want to give her a chance. Plus, I always wanted a hamster or something."

We threw question after question at her, as she diligently and excitedly wrote them down. "What does a hamster eat? Do they get along with other pets? How long do they typically live? Do they bite? How much do supplies cost?"

She grabbed her laptop and spent hours poring over the research. She of course wanted to present that day, but after asking more questions, it became apparent that she had to do more research. My husband firmly instructed that she spend time making the slides, and her sister gracefully assisted her with transitions. After she made approximately thirty slides, she declared she was ready to present them to the family.

What did my husband do? He told her to present after we returned from a week-long trip to visit our friends. When we returned from the trip, she had an additional ten slides. I encouraged her to practice and dress for success. It was adorable to hear her practicing with her room door closed.

The day arrived to present to us. She put on her "Daddy's My Hero" T-shirt and layered a "Best Sister" sweater on top. Prior to beginning the presentation, she showcased the sweater and peeled it off to reveal the T-shirt, declaring, "Extra points!" She then went through the forty-plus slides, five to six of which were items she would need to purchase, the cost, and review ratings out of five stars. At the end of the presentation, she thanked all her helpers, including Oz who had previously been convinced to help with the guinea pig and would get a companion, as the guinea pigs thrive in pairs. Ya Ya thanked us for giving her a chance, and her paternal grandmother for agreeing to take care of them when we go on vacation.

My mom, Oz, my husband, and I voted on pieces of paper; my husband declared that the decision had to be unanimous. I was worried because when my daughter first asked for the guinea pig, my mother was a hard NO. She refused to take care of the guinea pigs when we went on vacation. That led to a discussion with Ya Ya that she would need to include alternative caregivers for vacation in her presentation. I wrote down my "Yes" with a heart. Surprisingly, my mom wrote, "Yes, because your grandmother will watch them." Ya Ya jumped for joy. The next day, we proceeded to make accessories out of toilet paper rolls and cardboard to save money. My husband advised Ya Ya to look for potential pets following our three-week vacation to Asia.

When the family returned from summer vacation to Asia in July of 2023, Ya Ya was particularly interested in getting a teacup chihuahua because we went to dog cafes and pet stores. When she returned to school the following month, she said, "I'm stressed out. I don't think I could get a guinea pig. I still have to do my homework, Kumon, and go to jiu jitsu."

Oz comforted her, "It's only the first week," communicating to Ya Ya to get into a routine.

I mentioned, "You have to feel it out. Sometimes it's not the best time to get a pet."

As of publication, Ya Ya still has not decided if it is the right time.

Cancel the Filter

Life's Teachers

Two of the most harsh and instructive teachers of life lessons are loss and grief. Many people believe that bad things happen in threes or around the same time and use the phrase, *"When it rains, it pours!"* We were no exception to the adage. It started with a double whammy–a gastrointestinal flare-up with intense, raging pain and our fifteen-year-old dog coming through the dog door with his eye gushing blood. It looked as if his eye was poked by something sharp and he could not open it. I grabbed a cotton round to try to apply pressure, but he winced in pain. This little Pomeranian had a high pain tolerance, as evidenced by being bitten by a larger dog and clawed by a raccoon that came through the dog door in the past. The fact that he would barely let me near his eye was genuinely concerning. My husband contacted pet hospitals for any available appointments with one after the other indicating that they were booked until next week. He began calling emergency rooms, which were also backlogged. They directed him to sit in the waiting room until a doctor was available.

We had to decide whether our dog would go to the ER, or me. I encouraged my husband to take our dog while I stayed at home with the kids. He went to two hospitals, and when he was about to see a doctor, a dog was close to passing away, so he waited at the hospital for a total of seven hours before being seen. They then referred us to an ophthalmologist who recommended removing the eye, which would require expensive surgery. Either way, the eye was blind.

Fortunately, I am part of a community where I asked for recommendations for reputable veterinarians who are reasonably priced. We found an amazing doctor who recommended trying to salvage the eye with drops, which he could write prescriptions for, and the scripts could be filled at a local pharmacy. He did not try to gouge us with expensive bills but genuinely wanted to help our dog. He said that eye removal was not a specialized surgery, and he could perform it if needed at a way lower cost than a specialist. We will be forever grateful because the eye began to look like his eye, although still blind. Kindness goes a long way with us and others.

As my dog received his treatment, I was still in pain. My husband then dropped me off at the ER, as he could not go in with me due to COVID-19 protocol. I waited for a brief assessment and an available bed. The doctor assessed me, concluding that I had gastric pain, and the nurses gave me an IV and pain medication. Then, the doctor discharged me. I was grateful for the nurse because she demonstrated warmth, care, and concern, whereas the doctor was matter-of-fact, and seemed dismissive. I went home with no further insight and was recommended to be on a liquid diet. My friends were making bone broth and selling the jars, so my husband called them to ask if they had reserves. I am now sick of bone broth, despite it being delicious and saving my stomach.

My husband was a trooper, and I still feel guilty about him being available 24/7 for all of us, particularly as my kids started a new school year in 2021. I had to return to the ER the next day and spend the night because my stomach was not getting better. Several tests were done, and I was negative for an ulcer. They pumped me with morphine, and when I woke up, the doctor from the first day was there. I had lost a total of seven pounds on my already small frame, and I was given a prescription to cope with the acid and possible bacteria. I began taking a probiotic and ate fish and vegetables for months before being able to add some variety. The support of my husband was essential in nursing our dog and me back to health and getting the kids off to a good start.

The Worst Pain of My Life and I've Had Two C-Sections!

Even after two C-sections and living with IBS, I was not prepared to experience the intense pain that occurred when Mikey, our oldest fur baby's health began to deteriorate and he walked over the Rainbow Bridge. It seemed sudden, but maybe it wasn't because he was losing weight over the past few months. Mikey, our fur son, taught my husband and me to be parents. On 11/9/21, I heard him hack up yack, and I chalked it up to him eating something weird in the backyard or overstuffing himself with Ya Ya's homemade peanut butter treats or mildly stale cinnamon cereal given to us by my in-laws. But then I was surprised to wake up to one yellow, liquid puddle at the foot of our bed

Cancel the Filter

and one in the living room. During a work call, I scowled as I spotted three trails of puke on the couch. I frantically contacted my husband to come home to help me clean the mess, but he couldn't leave work until lunchtime. I put my arms and elbows into cleaning the beige couch, wrongly assuming that since the girls were older, gone were the days that I would be cleaning puke off it.

When I returned home from acupuncture, Mikey wasn't begging for food at lunch like usual. I placed him on my lap as I worked at the lunch table. He later did not eat dinner, and I took him near the water bowl because he hadn't drunk for hours. My husband took him to the front of the house to pee before bed. I thought the rancid smell that lingered on my sweater, blankets, and pillow was just a residual puke smell. He curled around my head, and I felt badly that the smell was so off-putting to me, especially because my nose was sensitive.

My husband decided to take Mikey to the vet the next morning. I went back to sleep, relieved that a doctor would examine him. I was awakened by an unfamiliar sight, my husband sobbing.

"Are you really crying?" I asked, hedging to see if he was just joking as he often does.

He nodded sullenly. "His organs are failing," he choked out.

"No! No! No!" I screamed and began sobbing.

"We have to decide when to put him down," he said.

The finality of that sentence sent guttural sobs throughout my body.

My mom came into our room and she began to cry.

I clutched and cuddled Mikey tightly, wailing, "I can't. I can't." At that moment, I realized that the bad smell was him slowly dying.

It's not like I didn't know this day would come, and somehow, I had a strange feeling that it would be in his seventeenth year. I just hoped it wouldn't happen this year or ever. I always thought when it did, we could spread his ashes in Santa Cruz at the park he played at and loved as a puppy. We would meet his friends there every day during college. My husband and I made plans to visit that park before taking him to the vet to rest. We wanted one more night with him.

I cried non-stop, telling him how much I loved him and how much he had done for me. That he didn't even know how much, although he did. He sniffed a piece of turkey lunch meat, licked it, the first time he even showed interest in food, but it was short-lived. I tried to put him near the tree where all the dogs peed, but he collapsed on the wet soil and mulch. I picked him back up to lay on the patio furniture in the sun, resting his head on a stuffed horse. At one point, he jolted up, likely hearing that annoying bee buzzing around my salad. I brought him back on the couch and told him again how hard it would be when I had to say goodbye. His eyes registered recognition and as I scanned his body, I observed that his stomach was turned inward, looking like skin and bones. He continued to twitch and grind his teeth. At one point, his top vampire tooth got stuck in the blanket, and I had to open his mouth to pull it free.

* * *

I got Mikey on my twentieth birthday. My friends had chipped in towards the $400 cost. My parents never let me have a dog growing up, only fish. In all fairness, we rented all our lives, and my mom was afraid of dogs because she was chased by one as a teen on her way home. However, I always hoped they would cave in and get me a Golden Retriever.

I remember cradling Mikey in a blanket on the ride back from his original home to our rental house. A grandma was selling a Chihuahua because her grandson tried to throw him off a balcony, which signaled he was either not old enough to own a dog or he should've been diagnosed with conduct disorder. The grandma told us that Mikey was a purebred Chihuahua, but as time progressed, he kept growing. Once, a boy said, "That's the biggest Chihuahua I've ever seen!"

We pulled over at a gas station to fill up and ironically, he puked, likely from motion sickness. When we got back to the house, we introduced him to our friends/roommates. We took Mikey down to our room and placed him in the dog bed the previous owner gave us. After a few nights of whining, my husband eventually gave in and let him sleep in bed with us. For seventeen years, he slept in our bed. But before his passing, he chose to sleep on the couch or a weighted blanket at the foot of our bed because age made it difficult for him to use the ottoman to

Cancel the Filter

get up onto the bed. In addition to whining, Mikey was crafty and smart and when we went to class or work, he would find a way out of his dog pen. He would drag it on top of his bed so he could slip under. Once, he got to my Reese's peanut butter cups and only ate the centers. He also loved Mr. Lion, a stuffed toy we won multiple times at a beach boardwalk, and would play tug of war with it.

Being our first fur baby, we enrolled him in the local pet store's training school. To this day, he is the only one of our dogs to graduate. Yet, he had several accidents while we were potty training. Fortunately, we had a brown carpet, and we did our best to make good use of a cleaner for pet urine. From that house, we moved to a townhouse with a solarium where he would sunbathe.

After graduation when we moved to Virginia for my graduate studies, Mikey took his first and only plane ride, stored under the plane in a crate. When we picked him up, we thought he peed everywhere, but he was dry heaving and salivating due to stress. We soon wanted to give him a brother and adopted Cokey, who was jumpy and likely abused before we adopted him. Once, I was walking both of them and Cokey slipped out of his collar. I told Mikey to stay, trusting him, or rather having to trust him because I had to chase Cokey through the forest. I eventually caught him, and when I got back to the apartment door, Mikey was faithfully still there. The training school really paid off!

Throughout graduate school, we moved multiple times, sometimes two times a year! When my brother moved in with us, he purchased a dog, and Mikey adjusted to his brother even though he was rambunctious and annoyed by him, as evidenced by Mikey's constant warning growls to stop bothering him. We eventually moved back to the Bay Area, moving multiple times as well. He also had numerous opportunities to run from my in-law's house when we lived with them. It's like he knew he had a good life. Once, we panicked because we couldn't find him, but he was just chilling on the front lawn. Another time, he left the house for our neighbor's house, likely following his younger brother for his own good.

Mikey has been there for every major life event—our two children being born, moving at least ten times, being broke throughout our education, to being my co-worker throughout the pandemic and snoring on my conference calls while I feigned being apologetic to the person on the other side of the screen. My human colleague often joked that he probably needed a CPAP machine.

* * *

The girls came back from school, wailing. My husband had picked them up early from school, and Oz knew right away that Mikey was dying. We all cried together as we hugged, cradled, and cuddled him. That night was long and sleepless. I was afraid to miss his last breath, but a part of me didn't want to hear it because it would mean he was physically gone. While we planned on taking him to the park, my husband and I knew that he would likely not make it. At one point, Mikey appeared overheated, and we laid him next to Cokey by the dog door. I then picked him up and put his face in the water bowl, and he took a few sips. My husband watched him until he woke us up at 5:00 a.m.

"He doesn't have much time left," he said gingerly.

I took Mikey into my arms and the girls, and my husband embraced us. Life slowly drained from his eyes, and it seemed he was holding on for as long as he possibly could. We were all sobbing as I told him, "It's okay. We love you. Go to bed bed now."

I will never forget the final look as his eyes bulged ever so slightly and then his eyes went lifeless, a slight tint of blue remained. For a while, we were unsure if he was gone or not because he gasped here and there, but it was likely his body's muscle memory. His mouth was slightly ajar, revealing his bottom teeth. Although I put his eyelids down, they kept coming up slightly. We watched a movie in bed together until his body could be taken to the vet for cremation.

Until the end, Mikey knew what we needed, and what he needed, which was to leave on his own terms and to ensure that we would be okay. We were together, feeling the love and pain together. I held him for almost an hour, never imagining I would hold him lifeless for that long. I wanted to pretend it wasn't true for just a while longer. When I glanced at his face though, I couldn't deny it.

We wrapped him in an Olaf blanket, but then I had to unwrap his head to take his collar off. I clutched it as I rewrapped him. Oz

Cancel the Filter

insisted on going with her father to hold him in the car. I knew I couldn't do it, or rather, I didn't want to. We gave Oz a choice and she did what I couldn't do. Later, I told her how brave she was. I clutched his collar until my fingers went white, sobbing as Ya Ya comforted me, parroting the line I said the day before, "He will always be in our hearts."

When they returned from the vet, my husband went from room to room, sobbing, "Everywhere I go reminds me of him."

Oz was sobbing, and I hugged my husband firmly, telling him he was such a good daddy. When I finally went to make tea, I looked around at the empty couch where less than twenty-four hours ago, we were all lying together, Mikey lying on my chest until he got too warm. His white hair was sprinkled on the couch and on my long-sleeve black shirt and sweatpants. I stared at his labs which indicated liver disease. I wondered if he had been sick for a while and his life could've been prolonged. I did not want my mind to go there because he lived a long, happy life.

Mikey was born for me. I was his person and he spread all his love, joy, and grumpiness to all of us. It seems cliché but he knew and waited until we said it was okay to let go. As my husband said, "He gave us one more night and held on for as long as possible."

I agreed because while his body was declining, his eyes registered clarity and recognition of what was going on. He was dizzy and weak, but he never lost his mental faculties and for that, I am grateful. My heart still hurts nonetheless while simultaneously taking comfort in being with him until the end.

We planned to spread his ashes at the park and place a picture of him on his box of ashes. My husband also wanted to take some of his ashes on vacation to Hawaii with us. I couldn't wail because I didn't want to upset the girls even more.

Ya Ya had difficulty understanding cremation, asking, "Why do we have to burn him? Why do we have to do that to him?" She always had faith that he would recover.

Her questions also made me question euthanasia. She would ask, "Why do we have to kill him?"

"They do that to humans, too," I reasoned, although only certain states even allow this. In the end, I'm relieved that he went on his own terms, unassisted by medications.

Mikey was such a good boy, my best friend, and fur son. Throughout his whole life, he stood by my side, lay on me, or next to me. He never judged or questioned me and loved me unconditionally. Our bond will be with me forever. Mikey even listened to me rehearsing my dissertation and job interview answers thousands of times. He would always look for me in my office so he could curl up in my lap. I would tell him, "Time to go to work." He must've been getting so tired because he didn't come to work as much towards the end. My co-worker put it best, "It's like a chunk of your heart is ripped out."

Joyful memories of Mikey from family and friends:

- In college, we surrounded the trash cans with dog pens so he couldn't get into the scraps. Once, he pulled the dog pen out and got lamb shank bones—his favorite. My husband tried to get them from him, and Mikey was out for skin!
- Mikey was known for spite peeing. If he knew we were going on vacation or a flight, he would pee on our suitcase. He would make it known when he wasn't happy, peeing on chair legs even though he could hold his pee like a champ. Sometimes, he would look you right in the eye, lift his leg, and let the yellow rain go as if he was saying, "You are fucking going to leave me?"
- Once we placed him in the shallow part of the ocean in college and he doggie paddled, giving us the look, "F*ck you, bitches!"
- We would use Mikey as a screener for our friends and roommates' dates. If he wanted to bite them it was a no-go.
- In grad school, we would open the door during Halloween and Mikey and the other dogs would be behind a dog pen. That was the trick because they would bark at the trick-or-treaters.
- Mikey would sit on a furry, white rug in my glam room as I got ready every day.

Cancel the Filter

- He danced for treats. Once my brother and his best friend kept telling him, "Dance, dance, dance," and he did. They gave him pizza crust.

Here is the eulogy I wrote for him on social media:

This morning we lost one of the loves of our lives. It seemed so sudden, one day Mikey was puking, the next we were told that his organs were failing him. We wanted one more night with him before taking him to the vet. Like the loving, faithful fur son he was, he continued breathing, despite having not eaten for three days. He took his last breath in my arms and everyone's arms wrapped around us. He traveled to the 🌈 bridge on his own terms, with his family.

Seventeen wonderful years. He helped my husband and me learn to be parents at a young age. This dog was born to be my best friend, biggest supporter, first fur son, and coworker, and he was the paragon of unconditional love. I mean, who else would listen to me practicing my dissertation a billion times?

We moved sometimes twice a year when I was a broke AF college/grad student. He accommodated two fur bros, two children who he meant the world to, and all our ups and downs over the years.

Our hearts are broken. I've never felt pain like this before. Every single place in the house reminds us of him. We cry solo and as a family. All I know is that we will continue to love you and Mommy will see you again someday 🙏 🖤 I cannot thank you enough or be grateful enough for all you have given us.

The grief continues to come in waves. I still lay in his spot on the couch to remember him. Immediately after his passing, I dreaded changing my clothes and bedding in fear that his fur and smell would disappear. I changed my computer screen to a picture of him lying in my lap during work and created a shared folder of pictures and videos with my husband. He was always there, his butt or his whole body, so embedded in our lives. I share this because this is the loss of a family member. You may not have a pet or lost a pet, but this grief is real. I am grateful for the outpouring of support from my friends and family. My friend sent me a comfort box with meditations to heal after loss. The waves will come, and you just have to ride them.

I Dig It

We had a vacation planned a couple of months after Mikey passed away in 2021. One of the ways I coped with my grief was by browsing adoption and puppy sites, which led to a family meeting about the possibility of getting a Golden Retriever puppy that I saw online. The seller responded to my email inquiry, stating that the Golden Retriever puppy was still available and even dropped the asking price by $350. The timing wasn't ideal because our vacation was ten days long, so my husband left it up to fate and negotiated another $100 off. However, the seller remained firm on the $350 reduction. Getting the kids involved in the decision appeared to be a mistake because it got our hopes up. Not to mention brainstorming names for the puppy which led to some joy and excitement, a much-needed reprieve from grief.

The next day, the puppy seller stated that she could reduce the cost by another $100! My husband and I knew that if we saw the puppy, he would be coming home with us. On the way to the pet store parking lot, we brainstormed names, and Biscuit or Breadstick was in the running. When we got there, the puppy was hanging out by the heater of the woman's passenger seat. He was such a sweet boy, and the seller stated that she would keep him if she could but she had a newborn. When we all hugged him and pet him, it was a done deal, but the names didn't seem to quite resonate with us any longer. Ya Ya suggested, Dug as in the Golden Retriever's name from the Disney Movie, *Up*. Side note, I didn't even know that dog was a Golden Retriever. Telling people his name always includes explaining the inspiration. Case in point, when my husband took Dug to a dog park and said his name, he heard someone mutter, "You might as well have just named him Bob."

Dug continued to be a sweet boy, and like any puppy, he teethed, nipped, and bit. We've always had small dogs, so these razor-sharp teeth combined with his size, which enabled him to jump on furniture, were new to us. Gone were the days when we could jump on our bed or couch to escape the biting. Not to mention his accidents were huge puddles. Fortunately, Goldens are highly intelligent, and he learned to use the dog door in a record, two days! Dug also stopped chewing and nipping, well, not completely. In fact, right before my podcast interview with an author, he chewed up the cover of the book! Fortunately, I already finished the book, but he couldn't even wait until the day after! According to the veterinarian, he is estimated to grow to be eighty to ninety pounds! Yikes!

Following Over the Rainbow Bridge

Four months after Mikey's passing, Cokey followed him over the Rainbow Bridge in 2022. We did not want to acknowledge his declining energy and body because he was still eating and drinking. However, he began losing control of his bowels and seemed constantly thirsty, spending his time standing next to the water bowl. After drinking, he would stare off into space. Other times when our puppy tried to play with him, he would snarl at him.

Then one day, after my dad and I returned from the pharmacy, I found poop in the house and my dad found Cokey passed out on one side. When my husband came home, we knew that Cokey didn't have much time. We wrapped him in a towel, kept calling the veterinarian, and went to pick up the girls from school. They knew something was immediately wrong when they saw us in the car.

The signs were clear, Cokey face-planted in his water bowl as his back legs gave way. My father took care of the girls as my husband and I drove to the vet, since I would not make the same mistake of letting my daughter accompany him instead of me. Even when you know it is the right decision, it still hurts. Thank the Buddha for our vet who always seems to accommodate us in times of need.

The lasting memory that I have of Cokey is him lying on his side, and the doctor administering the injection that would lead him to the Rainbow Bridge. Cokey has always been a fighter, and his seven-to-eight-pound body fought to continue breathing. The vet slowly injected another shot, and then Cokey stilled. We hugged and kissed him, and my husband covered his body with the towel, his head still visible. *Our little.* We told the girls that he passed at the hospital. We learned not to say, "We put him down," because from their perspective, that means we caused his death rather than made a choice to end his suffering. The intent is different, but this nuance was hard to explain to them. This did not reduce the overarching sadness that we felt. On St. Patrick's Day, Oz was screaming, puking, and having panic attacks. Her grandpa soothed her, rubbing her back as she puked, telling her not to make herself sick.

What do you do when your entire family feels like shit? Have an arcade day at Dave & Buster's! My husband also told the girls that they didn't have to do Kumon or homework. Personally, I continued to struggle. I went through the motions of driving them to a birthday tea party, going to Korean class, and working. I was hesitant to take time off because we had two vacations planned. In hindsight, it would have been better for my mental health if I had done so. I also became even more lenient during this time, fulfilling Oz's request for the shortest haircut she ever had. It is extremely hard to absorb your children's pain and process your feelings simultaneously. The sadness just hangs over everyone like a dark cloud.

Many people don't understand or know what to say when a person passes, let alone when fur babies cross the Rainbow Bridge. However, some people know exactly how you feel, and that included my dear friend, Priscilla Azcueta, whose fur baby passed the year before Cokey. She dropped off flowers, stuffed animals, and a card to offer her condolences. She empathized with my observation that sitting around the house, you notice their presence everywhere—their water bowls, favorite spots to sunbathe, nap, and cuddle, and ashes in boxes with their pictures on them, which remind you that their bodies were reduced to particles by fire. The pain is palpable, and Oz's sensitivity and irritability were heightened, becoming upset over seemingly minor things.

I wish I could tell you that time will make your grief go away, but for those who have lost someone significant in their lives, it comes in waves. However, there are support systems and professionals that can be a great support. For Oz, we encouraged her to take time off school on days when she felt extreme difficulty concentrating. She cried at school and her friends supported her as well. Oz also met with a child psychologist for several sessions, exploring coping strategies for grief, anxiety, and sadness. After much internal deliberation, I attended a free grief support group for pet loss, which was cathartic for me because I was able to cry in front of strangers. While I cried in front of them, I did not completely let the rain from my eyes loose, particularly since Oz was having panic attacks. Members comforted me and said that Oz going to Mikey's euthanization did not directly lead to her having panic attacks or contribute to how she was responding to the loss of Cokey.

Hearing others' stories facilitates empathy and gratitude. Two of the members' dogs were diagnosed with cancer which led to imminent death. Another felt that the vet misdiagnosed her fur baby, and she did not have the financial means for cremation. One of the members' dogs jumped off the dashboard out of the car window, which sounded absolutely devastating. Another member's dog and bird passed away, and she considered them her only family. The average age of the deceased fur babies was approximately eleven to twelve years old, and one person stated, "You are lucky. I wish my babies lived sixteen to seventeen years." The members gave me a safe space to express my feelings of pain and helplessness about Oz's grief response, which I could not absorb or take away, but gave her space to feel. They also helped me realize that I was able to experience Mikey and Cokey's presence, love, and unconditional love for a very long time, by sharing so many positive memories with them. I am also extremely lucky that I have a loving family that provides each other with mutual love and support. It makes a huge difference when you are experiencing life lessons, especially the hard ones.

Grief is a continual process, and I will continue to honor their lives and memories. One way I did so was to work with a Korean American artist who completed detailed tattoos of their faces with unique collars, and now, I have them permanently memorialized on my arm to look at them anytime.

Stephanie J. Wong

The Kobe Bryant Tragedy

On January 26, 2020, we were in the Jacksonville, Florida airport, getting ready to return home. As the girls and I were looking around an airport store, my husband sharply said, "Oh shit." I thought he was irritated that our flight was delayed because it is pretty uncharacteristic of him to use profanity, and even less uncharacteristic to say it loudly in a public place.

"What's wrong?"

"Kobe Bryant just died," he said frantically.

"Is it true?" I was a bit skeptical because there is often fake news about celebrities passing.

"Looking it up now," he said.

It was then reported by TMZ that Kobe died in his private helicopter along with five other people. While TMZ may seem like a gossip website and show, they are typically never wrong. As the story unfolded, it was later revealed that Kobe and Vanessa Bryant's thirteen-year-old daughter, Gianna, died in the crash with Kobe. She and Kobe were traveling to a game at Kobe's Mamba Sports Academy. The story became even more tragic when the final report revealed seven other deaths.

The tragic deaths shook the NBA universe and the world. Kobe was merely forty-one years old and Gianna was a teenager and rising basketball star. He was survived by his three other daughters and wife, his youngest daughter being seven months old. Celebrities, fans, and civilians expressed grief and sadness. The 2020 Grammy Awards was hosted at Staples Center, also known as the "House that Kobe Built." Alicia Keys was the perfect person to pay homage to the legend and exude compassion and love.

My husband took the tragedy the hardest, stating that no celebrity death had ever hit him as hard as Kobe's death. My husband wasn't a Lakers fan, but he admired Kobe's accomplishments on and off the court. My husband sent me Sports Center Correspondent Elle Duncan's tribute to Kobe, where she recalled her interaction with Kobe. It was during her pregnancy, and Kobe immediately asked her the sex of the baby. She told him it would be a girl, and he told her that girls are a blessing, and labeled himself a Girl Dad, as all his children are girls and

Cancel the Filter

he loved it that way. I think this resonated most with my husband who is a Girl Dad himself. He believed that Kobe and Gianna were going to advance female sports.

My husband spent days watching tribute videos, feeling overwhelming grief. I tried to comfort him, and told him, "What makes you think Kobe and Gianna won't advance female sports?" A few days after their deaths, Vanessa Bryant took to Instagram to share her message, which of course expressed her and her family's overwhelming sadness. She also continued to advocate for the Mamba Academy and shared news of the new Mamba Three Fund to help the families of the others who passed in the crash.

Since that day, my husband said he has been more tolerant of our girls' behaviors. He tends to be the one to maintain rules and be more assertive when it comes to whining or the beginnings of a tantrum. In my book (no pun intended), Kobe has changed more than the landscape of women's sports, he has set the tone for how we should treat our daughters. He has also communicated to the world that life is too short, and we should embrace our loved ones and opportunities to be great.

Cancel the Filter on Traveling

A Worldly Education and Global Perspective

A common fear that people communicate when they are deciding whether or not to have a child is they won't be able to travel. The subtext is that they will be restricted to their home for years with no social life or flexibility to do things they want to do. Not going to lie, this often happens, but you can consciously decide to travel with your kids. Is it annoying to pack up loads of shit like car seats and strollers? Absolutely! So, why do we travel when there are so many inconvenient aspects? Why do we bring our kids and groom them to be globetrotters? Trevor Noah puts it best, "Traveling is the antidote to ignorance."

Growing up, the farthest my parents ever took me for vacation was to Los Angeles, an approximately six-hour drive from the Bay Area. Firstly, they never had the desire to travel, and I don't think they knew the logistics of flying long distances. Looking back at it, another factor was that my father was the sole income provider in our family so we did not grow up with excess funds to go on extravagant vacations. I was unaware of what was out there beyond the Bay Area and Los Angeles.

Fast forward to when I grew up: I wanted to travel everywhere. Now, I am not the back-pack-around-the-world, hostel-staying type. I wish I were! Regardless, my husband and I have three priorities when we travel— eat delicious food, engage in fun activities, and relax. The three priorities were passed down to Oz and Ya Ya and when we go on vacation, we make a list of all the things we want to do. My husband then groups activities that are in close proximity and sees what days and times we could realistically do the activities. Basically, my husband is the family's travel agent, but does not have a formal, set schedule. Instead, each day, we all discuss what we feel like doing and what neighborhood we

Cancel the Filter

would like to explore. Of course, there are activities where we have to book a reservation, but all the other days and times are flexible. The only difference between the way we travel as a couple and as a family is that there are more people to contribute to the fun.

For example, traveling in our early and mid-20s looked like this: Flying with friends to Cabo San Lucas or Puerto Vallarta. We tended to rent a large suite for six of us to share. One couple in the group would eat ramen to save money, in addition to walking in the heat versus taking a taxi. We drank cheap drinks, danced, and during one trip, had racist comments thrown our way. On one trip to Cabo San Lucas, we went to a restaurant outside of the tourist area. Before we could even enjoy the complimentary tortilla chips, an older woman began to dance around our table. My husband told her that we were just trying to enjoy our meal. She returned dancing and ate a chip from our basket.

"Hey!" my husband firmly said, glancing back at the woman's table.

"Chinks, go back to China," she seethed.

I'll never forget the hate in her eyes as she said this statement. It cut to my core because I couldn't understand how she could hate someone so much based on their appearance.

"I'm not Chinese," my husband calmly replied.

He was met with a punch across his cheek.

Screaming ensued with one of the woman's friends yelling at my husband, "You're a man, you should just take it [the punch]."

The woman again told my husband to go back to China and he provided the same response. He eventually looked to the woman's partner, telling him, "Get her out of here."

During the entire interaction, no one moved inside the restaurant. I wondered if they were used to this kind of behavior, or if they didn't see it as their business to intervene. Either way, we finished our dinner and went back to the rental. I learned a life lesson that racism and discrimination can unfortunately be experienced anywhere.

While traveling in our early thirties with Oz and Ya Ya looked like this: Poop on a plane, in reference to *Snakes on a Plane* starring Samuel L. Jackson.

Oz was close to ten months old when my husband and I took her on a flight to the East Coast for a friend's wedding. The poor girl ended up having a fever. We rushed her to the ER with our friends who we were staying with, and the nurses must have poked her arm over ten times with a needle because they could not find her small veins to insert the IV. As a parent, I felt helpless that there was nothing I could do to make her feel better. We had to leave that hospital to go to a pediatric specialist who was able to insert the IV. Due to Oz having a fever, the nurse suggested that Oz should only have a diaper on. Then another female patient in the waiting room began to whisper to the nurse, asking if she assessed whether we hit our child. *Judgmental much?* The nurse calmly responded that they were Mongolian birthmarks on her back, which are common among Asian babies, and fade with time. I wanted to hug the nurse for being so culturally sensitive because our pediatrician at home said the same thing.

When we were discharged from the hospital, my poor daughter had her entire arm wrapped in gauze and was not given a specific diagnosis. She continued to have a fever, so my husband stayed at our friend's house with her, while my best friend and I enjoyed a gorgeous Asian-Indian American wedding.

On our flight back to the Bay Area, my husband, the Baby Whisperer, was carrying Oz in the Bjorn as he took them both for a walk down the aisle. Oz was clearly still not feeling like herself. Suddenly, there was a pungent smell coming from him and Oz. As a rule of thumb, I asked my husband if he farted. He denied it and proceeded to, as most parents do, smell the baby's bottom. The result: Poop on his hand, which had seeped out of her diaper into the carrier, and onto him! He jolted up and bee-lined for the restroom. He frantically instructed, "Get me some clothes!"

I rushed back to the overhead compartment and then back to him. "There aren't any clean clothes."

"Get me anything! Anything smells better than smelling like shit!"

Point well taken.

Traveling in our 30s with our kids typically included two strollers, five suitcases, two backpacks, stuffed animals, and a bag for snacks. If it was only my husband and me traveling together, the load was much lighter and we reverted back to our three travel priorities without having to consider how family-friendly the activities or restaurants were. Since

Cancel the Filter

2016, I have made it my goal to take one big trip a year with my family. In 2016, I went to Thailand with my husband. In 2017, I traveled to Japan and Korea with the kids, and my husband, mother, and brother. Then in 2018, Barcelona and Paris with the kids, my husband, and my in-laws. The kids flew back to the US with their grandparents, and my husband and I went on to Greece. In 2019, we went to the Philippines and South Korea.

Let me paint a picture for you of our 2019 trip. Seven-year-old Oz is pushing a medium-sized suitcase and I am pushing a large suitcase while carrying a backpack and snack bag. The large suitcase contained protein powder and Girl Scout cookies for our friend who resided in Korea. My husband was pulling three suitcases on a somewhat busted dolly, in addition to tucking one stroller under each arm. Four-year-old Ya Ya was solely responsible for following us with her stuffed animal, and it was very difficult for her to not drop her stuffed animal. Now I understand why Kevin got lost in *Home Alone*.

In hindsight, there were too many transportation changes on the trip. The drive from Manila Airport to the hotel took an hour. We then spent one day in Manila and took a four-hour drive to Cebu where we stayed for a few days. We subsequently went back to Manila Airport to fly to Incheon in South Korea. From there, we took a one-hour bus ride to Seoul, which was followed by another one-hour bus ride to our friend's house. We stayed overnight and then took a two-to-three hour bus ride to Busan for a weekend trip. We returned to our friend's house to take our belongings to Seoul, and ultimately back to the airport after one-to-two days. We did all of this while carrying a ton of shit! Although I was able to dump the protein powder and cookies, I ended up replacing them with a shitload of beauty products, stuffed animals, etc.

Pro tip: If you need to take a taxi in South Korea, and you are traveling with a family and the accompanying luggage, you must call a jumbo taxi. You will need to identify the phone number and learn to book one. If you are at a hotel, they could do so for you, or nowadays, many Airbnbs have transportation to and from the airport included in your stay. If you do not choose one of these options, you will be at the mercy of a nice person who agrees to squeeze you into a regular taxi.

Despite the hassles and fatigue that also accompany traveling, we typically allow our kids to add another week to their spring break because they experience new places and interact with culturally diverse individuals. They also get to see that not all children are afforded the same opportunities. For example, in Manila and Cebu, many children buy water from the grocery store and walk alongside cars sitting in traffic, selling the water for a ten-cent markup, all while it is scorching-ass-hot!

In Cebu, we got to experience the kindness of those we interacted with and observe that many are trying to make an honest living, and not cheat you. Outside our hotel, we met Samuel, a driver of a jitney. We liked him so much that we asked him to drive us the next day, but he explained that it was his friend's turn to drive because they had a rotation. There was no hustle. There was no, "You are my client." It was, "It's your turn [friend]."

The other bonus was that Oz got to write about her trip for her first-grade project, entitled, "Trip to the Falls." We hiked the Kawasan Falls, a place so gorgeous that in person, it looks like a picture. As you hike up the mountains, one waterfall leads to another and another. At the second waterfall, my husband jumped off the mini cliff. My kids each jumped off twice. So, I couldn't "be a p*nis" as Trevor Noah would say, replacing the derogatory term for female genitalia because, from his perspective, women are stronger. So, I jumped off the cliff for the first time ever. Oz was able to write and draw about the hike and jumps, which is a memory that she will have forever.

Now, this trip was not all waterfalls and private drivers. There was exhaustion, the kids being picky about food, sunburn, swarms of bugs, and the kids breaking a lamp because they were throwing a squishy around. It was my husband and me pushing them in strollers in the scorching heat at an outdoor market, helping all of us adjust to the time differences, and my husband and I caring for the kids when they got fevers and coughs.

However, these are the memories that I live for. This is the quality time that you can never replace with time on your phone or sitting at a computer. It does not stop me from becoming grouchy during the trip from time to time (I'm human), particularly when they're riding two

Cancel the Filter

suitcases together like a skateboard because Oz wasn't feeling well enough to push one. I will pay this price for experiences like these.

Our 2018 trip to Barcelona and Paris taught us a valuable lesson: Do not assume your children can walk everywhere during the vacation or even most of the time, especially with the time difference. During this trip, we learned about melatonin from another parent, but it was too late to use it on this trip. The kids could not adjust to the time difference, and fell asleep like clockwork in the afternoon, which is prime time for eating and site-seeing. My father-in-law and my husband switched off carrying Oz, and my father-in-law and I switched off carrying Ya Ya.

One day, we planned to go to the top of the Eiffel Tower, and Oz said, "Let's walk up there!"

"Heck no! You cannot stay awake walking around the Parisian streets! I can't carry you guys up the Eiffel Tower!"

She resigned to take the elevator.

Pro tip: Bring strollers! For our 2019 trip, we got two free strollers from a neighborhood website. We eventually trashed them before coming back home, but it was worth lugging them around for as long as we did, or how else would we have navigated the busy streets of Myeong-dong in Korea?

Observation: It is hard to navigate with strollers in Tokyo, Japan. The birth rate has been declining and space-consciousness equates to small places. The space on the bus that is reserved for strollers is also reserved for wheelchairs. However, if you have small children, I would still recommend bringing them!

In 2022, we took our first international trip since the mandated shelter-in-place had us hunkering down. We traveled to Cabo with our friends who also have two daughters. We later went to Paris. In Cabo, we ate and went to the pool, whereas Paris was an eight-day excursion! This time, Oz and Ya Ya remembered their experiences, unlike the trip we took in 2018.

The Parisian trip kicked off with both families meeting at the airport. My husband had high hopes that we would be able to spend time at the lounge prior to boarding. However, one of the people at the front desk denied us entry with our priority pass because these cards apparently classified us as the peasants of luxury. As a result of not being a VIP member, we could not even slip in for some quick bites or refreshments. Another customer was allowed into the lounge, and we weren't sure if he was a VIP or not. The front desk person noted that we could order items at the desk to the left of him, so we ordered hella sandwiches, chips, and drinks. The person who was helping us kept darting her eyes between us and the front desk person who was clearly unhappy that she gave us all those snacks.

Later, my husband attempted again to walk in alone and get refreshments, but he was *denied*. The front desk person told him that they opened at 3:00 p.m., and we were boarding at 3:15 p.m. Since we ended up boarding later, my husband ran back to get food and refreshments. The front desk person tried to turn him away again, stating, "It is too close to boarding time."

The other employee let my husband in, but the front desk person kept following him around. While shoving various finger foods in his mouth, my husband spun around and said, "Just leave me alone and stop being a d*ck. You have to be nicer to people."

The flight was smooth enough, but the time difference was a bit rough. A tip at the airport: Don't hire folks approaching you inside the airport, claiming they are taxi drivers. The actual taxi drivers are outside in a small lot.

We stayed with our friends in a three-bed apartment in Vincennes, which was posted on Airbnb as a three bedroom and three bath. The apartment had three rooms, three showers, and three sinks, but only *one* toilet for eight people. We hilariously announced our bathroom needs and some of us accidentally walked in on each other. Our friend's daughter got stuck in the bathroom twice because the lock wouldn't budge. So, we made it a rule that when we were doing our business, we would not lock the door. The upside was that we stayed in Vincennes, which is a cute neighborhood with a bus station one-and-a-half blocks away. The train system is very efficient and affordable, and we took it everywhere. There was also a Monoprix across the street and it was

Cancel the Filter

glorious because they displayed pastries in the front window and baguettes were one euro and all types of deli meats were two euros!

The first and last night, we ate at Olympe Sport Café where the bartender, server, and owner were extremely friendly. The duck confit and au gratin potatoes and the filet mignon were wonderful and extremely affordable at fifteen euros. The server was a sweet woman who showed genuine interest in where we visited since the first night, and gave us suggestions. Funny enough, when Oz went outside, she felt like she needed to puke, which she did! She tends to be a puker when she eats too much or quickly. My husband then decided to affectionately throw disgusting-tasting pink candy and hit my head. All the kids started chasing him, throwing candy at him. "Justice for Stephanie," they screamed. Oh, good times!

The great thing about Paris is that there are bakeries every few blocks. Pro tip from a local: Look for artisan bakeries because it means the bread is fresh. In our neighborhood, my husband and I walked around the neighborhood and bought delicious shawarma on pita for six euros, and a small chocolate tart with gold flakes for our friend's birthday for 2,80 euros! When we arrived, the dollar was slightly stronger than the euro, but on the last day, the euro was slightly more than USD. Fortunately, my husband and I bought my luxury goods before the last day.

One of the best experiences of my life was at Chanel. I never could have dreamed that I would ever be able to buy anything from Chanel. In my youth, I realized the different classifications of socioeconomic status, and I wasn't in the upper echelon. While we waited a bit for a personal shopper, I tried on a black, sparkly long coat on display. The security guard then informed me that I cannot try clothes off the rack. So, despite the oohs and ahhs of my family, I put it back on the hanger, and like my own clothes, accidentally buttoned it in a misaligned fashion (pun intended).

Then Florence the personal shopper appeared with a dressing room. She assessed my style based on what I initially requested. She next walked past the jacket I hung up and said, "That looks a bit weird." Then shrugged and said, "I'll fix it later."

I have never had a personal shopper before. Florence treated me like a VIP, bringing out a jacket from the new winter collection. It was pink, looked like it had ruffled ribbons everywhere, and was priced at $7,500! I almost fainted. I tried on two tank tops, one of which I purchased. I tried on a $2,500 T-shirt and the quality was like no other T-shirt I've ever tried on or owned. Who buys a T-shirt for $2,500? I fell in love with boots with gold lettering, spelling out Chanel. I also tried on a midriff navy knit with a cherry pattern, and a baby blue tweed jacket, which made my shoulders puff up like a linebacker. My daughters filmed me as I walked out of the dressing room, I felt like a million bucks. Money opens doors and Florence was genuinely friendly and attentive, never appearing to look down on us, despite not being clad in designer clothes upon entering the store. When my husband asked if she had seen VIPs she responded, "Every customer is a VIP." This is the type of customer service that is a gold standard because everyone wants to be seen the way Florence makes you feel seen.

I also totally understand why people get addicted to shopping. When I was trying on all these clothes, adrenaline was rushing through me, and I was trying to convince myself that I could purchase them if I wanted to. My practical, logical brain compromised and concluded that I could purchase items, but they had to be staples. I was thinking about buying a brooch but decided against it since I had this magical experience and purchased a tank top and boots.

My husband had to return to the store to get the paperwork for a value-added tax (VAT) refund. Pro tip: At some stores, if your total is a specific amount or higher, you will receive a refund for these taxes as a foreigner. Therefore, if you are going to buy luxury goods, purchase them where there is a VAT refund! Another tip: Luxury stores will turn people away at a certain time and point in line. You want to try to get there as early as possible. Definitely, not near closing time unless you are a celebrity and/or uber-rich.

I had a sneaking suspicion that my husband would buy me the brooch because he is that thoughtful and sweet. Later in the day, he kept trying to offer me water, but I showed him that I was carrying a bottle. He got impatient and opened his backpack to reveal a teeny-tiny Chanel bag. I jumped into his arms. Prior to me opening it, he prefaced it with, "I'm not sure it is the right one." My face dropped because it wasn't the

Cancel the Filter

same one and I felt really bad that I hurt his feelings. I tend to wear my heart on my sleeve, and it wasn't a small purchase that you could keep and just buy another one. On our last night, he waited an hour and a half to see Florence again and she helped us exchange it without losing any money with the day's exchange rate.

In contrast to Florence, there are some customer service representatives whose perceptions are not as favorable. One of our friends got turned away from Rolex, telling him, "Nothing is for sale. Where are you from?"

He replied, "The US."

They said, "Buy it there."

The adage is true, "You can't judge a book by its cover." My friend dropped thousands on a ring for his wife at Cartier. He also used to be a pro skater and was treated like a VIP at the Supreme store. No one should be treated poorly because someone makes a negative judgment about them, and all people should be able to look/browse.

In France, I had zero migraines, which indicated that the root of many of my medical issues might be due to stress. When you are in Montmarte, strolling and looking at knick-knacks and sites, there is a sense of calm that washes over you. I was so excited to see La Maison Rose, a film site in *Emily in Paris*. I even wore my lavender beret to take a picture. By the way, these berets annoy many locals. When I sat down, the owner said, "No, no." She tilted the chairs towards the table to make them non-functional.

"I guess we are not eating here," I said.

"No, you're not," she replied.

My mouth hit the ground. We were legitimately going to eat at the restaurant, but apparently, we were not welcome.

After hours of walking, we finally found Le Chat Noir (the Black Cat) whose staff was able to accommodate us. We ate beef bourguignon and lamb shank near the Red Light District. The servers were extremely nice and even apologized for the La Maison Rose incident!

On another night, we went to Chez Pippo due to Florence calling the restaurant and speaking in French. Prior to Florence's help, we placed a reservation online, but it kept getting canceled. Restaurants usually close between lunch and dinner so the earliest you can eat is at

7:00 p.m., and the only time we could get in was at 10:00 p.m. Mango sorbet and pistachios were barely holding us over. At the restaurant, we ordered Cacio e Pepe with goat cheese, gnocchi with prosciutto, La Suprema pizza with spicy sausage, and pappardelle with Bolognese sauce. The food was delicious and the only thing that knocked down my overall review was that they charged us six euros per water bottle without telling us until we got the check for thirty-six euros. When we informed the manager, he deducted four euros.

Tourist highlights of our trip:

- Chinatown, which is more like Vietnamese town due to all the restaurants.
- Eiffel Tower at night
- Arc de Triomphe
- Le Marais (neighborhood)
- Sacré-Coeur
- Louvre (a bit crowded and stuffy for my taste this time); Ya Ya also got scared of the Mona Lisa because the eyes seem to follow you wherever you go. The fun fact is that it is insured for over $800 million! The painting was once stolen and the thief implicated Picasso as an accomplice.
- Champs Elysees
- Latin Quarter (Shakespeare and Company Bookstore)
- Panthéon
- Notre-Dame (this time saw it from afar because it was being rebuilt)
- Seine River
- Other delicious restaurants:
- L'as du Falafel
- Sanukiya-Karaage Ramen and black sesame mochi (owned by twins, one of which says he's better looking)
- La Scarpetta for lasagna
- Mimi Ramen (just don't bring in your lasagna and eat it)
- Pierre Hermé for macarons

You may have finished reading these travel stories, and think, *It's*

Cancel the Filter

easy to travel when you have money. I don't disagree. I work long hours almost everyday and my husband finds deals so we can take these trips. Some ways we save money include monitoring ticket prices for flights, being flexible on your departure and arrival dates/times, using budget airlines, bringing your own snacks and food on the plane, negotiating with Airbnb owners on their rental prices, and renting a space that has a washer/dryer so you don't have to pack a lot of clothes. But, even if you don't travel internationally, visiting a nearby town, city, and state will provide you with new experiences and you can observe the culture—ways people interact, local food that is prepared and sold, the pace of lifestyle, and leisure activities. These experiences remind you that you can still enjoy traveling even with children and they will likely grow up with open hearts and minds.

Cancel the Filter on Coronavirus (in a Cardi B. voice)

Like the rest of the world, shelter in place was in full effect in 2020 and changed our lives significantly. Beginning on March 17, 2020, I sheltered in place with my family and adapted to the life changes in work, relationships, and society. Let's cancel the filter that you were the only one who almost lost their shit every twenty seconds.

Luckily, I earned the right doctorate because I was able to see my patients via telehealth and not be at high risk of exposure. My husband was allowed to work from home three days per week. He went into the office at 7:30 a.m. and returned home by 10:00 a.m. to work the rest of the day. My mom continued to go to one of her jobs because she was considered an essential worker. All in all, COVID-19 revealed several life lessons to me:

- There was a new "normal."
- Teachers need to be paid and appreciated 1,000 times more than they are.
- Living with loved ones, particularly in times of shelter-in-place and social distancing, is a blessing.
- You can see how people react in times of stress—the good, bad, and ugly come out.
- Being a parent during these times was even more challenging because you had to be a teacher, parent, employee, boss, etc.
- There is such a thing as screen fatigue.
- Alcohol intake skyrocketed.
- Knowing your limits as a mental health provider is essential to self-care.

Cancel the Filter

Who would have thought in our lifetime that the primary mode of communication would be video conferencing (e.g., Zoom, Google Meet)? I like seeing my patients via video, which is a nice surprise for me. I enjoy working from home because my biggest barrier in the morning is leaving the house. I'm the one who is trying to find my office keys while grabbing a quick breakfast (Eggo waffles were my go-to), heating my tea, and packing anything in my rolling backpack that I may have forgotten. After the lockdown, the rush to do all of these things disappeared from my mornings. I now have easy access to all of my necessities. I think many people realized during the pandemic that many jobs and tasks can be done virtually.

Without in-person human interaction though, so much is lost, including not being able to see loved ones, hurting our eyes from an increase in screen time, experiencing more isolation, and struggling with the overlap between work and home, possibly leading to depression and anxiety. Sadly, my children had to see their paternal grandparents and my father through the window because they were in the high-risk population of contracting the disease. Not to mention socializing for children is essential for their development as human beings, and I never imagined that they would be video chatting so early in their lives. Not being in their classrooms with their teachers is not how I envisioned Ya Ya's kindergarten and Oz's second-grade experiences.

I am extremely grateful that I am an essential worker, and that our family has income. With that said, homeschooling our children was very challenging. In the beginning of the pandemic, the lesson plans provided by the teachers had to be implemented by the caregivers because there were no teleconferences yet. Then parents and caregivers began providing feedback to the teachers: We were about to lose our minds. They then implemented weekly Zoom meetings for Ya Ya and three times a week for Oz. This helped, but we were still primary teachers. The first week was the pits because we were doing classwork and homework till 4 p.m. every day, and they still had to do Kumon after school, or as comedian Jimmy O. Yang joked, "Asian children's prison." Overall, there was no structure during this time, and the readjustment period was driving me up the wall.

After the first week, we started to get in a groove. We were finishing most of the classwork before lunch, and Kumon began doing Zoom sessions. Seriously, if anyone who is not a pervert wanted to teach my children something useful, I would be all for it! I enlisted my uncle to help Ya Ya with journal entries. This was challenging because he did not know how to fully use the technology to see the picture message with the assignment and video chat. However, it was nice to have a senior citizen and a young person interacting during these difficult times.

Social distancing or standing six feet away from each other became the new protocol. People following it was another thing. Wearing masks in public was also implemented, and it was a tossup whether people wore them either. It was hard to not be able to invite neighbors, friends, or family over when you had a bit of free time. Luckily, we were a full house and my previous woes of having a hectic household with three adults, two children, and prior to Mikey and Cokey's walks over the Rainbow bridge, three dogs, were no longer an issue because we were never bored. For example, my children announced a weekly dog show competition. They each trained one dog, and one of us adults also trained one dog, while the other two adults served as judges. Oz trained one dog to jump through the hula hoop and my youngest looked like she was doing a ballroom dance with one of the dogs! I arrogantly stated, "My dog is the only obedience school graduate." Let's just say I got booted off the stage.

Every day, we were doing some activity and my favorite was karaoke time! There is nothing more stress relieving to me than singing a BTS or Blackpink song between meetings. My husband and I also competed weekly on the amount and intensity of our workouts, as measured by our smartwatches. He purchased a knockoff Peloton stationary bike, which he affectionately calls Beleton.

Now, you may be rolling your eyes, and saying to yourself, I did not have time for that because I was busier than I was before the shelter-in-place. I felt that way, too. I was only able to push through this because of my support system. My husband cooked all the meals, and we tagged each other in when we reached our home-schooling or meeting limit. I knew that we had each reached our limit when we had that irritable tone with the kids. The kids ate lunch and played with their friends on video chat when they were not doing academic work. Honestly, the rhythm

Cancel the Filter

had to do less with being able to handle the situation better, and more with acceptance that this was crazy! More chaos was the new normal, and we were all trying our best to make it through. Additionally, many people lost their jobs, did not have food, and couldn't pay their rent or mortgage. It helped put things in perspective for me that it could be worse!

This was truly a time when people were challenged to grow from adversity and not everyone was rising to the occasion, whereas others were demonstrating extremely kind behavior. There was no manual for how to deal with a pandemic; that may be a good second book. As a result, I had to interact with leaders and colleagues who hid, withdrew, and sharply responded. I didn't blame them, but I must acknowledge my disappointment. I am also guilty of having had a less-than-kind tone many times throughout this process while attempting to communicate ways to protect others' health. Being a leader who was true to my core belief of helping others, including my family, was not an easy feat nor was there an absence of frustration. Add being hard on yourself to the frustration, and it became difficult to restrain myself from having an attitude. This challenged me to examine my leadership style, communication skills, and beliefs, and to recover from missteps to improve my skills. At a time when the social divide was even more apparent, it was important to, as Brené Brown says, "...step into the arena of vulnerability." I do not have all the answers, but I'm going to fight for those that are marginalized.

One of our weekly traditions during the pandemic was watching John Krasinski's YouTube show, "Some Good News," highlighting acts of kindness and just good fun. It reminded us that not everyone was committing asinine behavior, or complaining about the lack of toilet paper and hand sanitizer, but rather many were supplying these essentials to others. It didn't hurt to see the Jonas Brothers at a virtual prom either.

Homeschooling

Let me start by saying, it was a privilege for our children to receive high-quality education and have access to the technology required to go to school during the pandemic. Some children and students needed to hover around Starbucks for Wi-Fi and were unable to obtain the necessary equipment to attend virtual school. What we learned from homeschooling was that our children missed their friends and the human interaction with their teachers very much. As humans, we need to see each other and be able to give each other hugs. The virus robbed them of the ability to run around the yard, play non-virtual games, and be present with each other. Teachers and students alike had Zoom fatigue, but Oz's fourth-grade teacher increased her enthusiasm on Zoom more than baseline because she wanted to keep the children energized. I heard it every day outside of my room as she encouraged them to do physical education exercises and work together to learn new things. The curriculum that I was most impressed by as a psychologist was about mindfulness, meditation, and a growth mindset. How great would it have been for me to learn that as a child? The two things that I learned in middle school that I still use today are sewing a hidden stitch and typing without looking at the keyboard.

For the most part, my family and I were able to adjust to the virtual model. Oz was old enough and conscientious by nature to maintain concentration and engagement. In contrast, by nature, Ya Ya is a ball of energy that if contained, bounces around everywhere. When Ya Ya was online with her class, the teacher reminded the students to stay engaged, but they were first graders. They also had more flexibility and autonomy to work on their homework than they would during an in-person lesson. These little kids had to use an app to complete their assignments and submit them. The teacher would then return the homework if there were corrections, or if the assignments were incomplete. One day, my husband noticed Ya Ya was getting work returned and asked her about it. He reviewed it and it was not written at all. For one of the assignments, she took a picture of her face and submitted it!

"Why did you do that?" my husband asked.

"I didn't want to do it [the assignment]," she pouted.

Cancel the Filter

My husband's stern talk in an exasperated tone, fortunately, ensured that this would not happen again. When I heard that the scolding was over, I pulled him aside and started laughing hysterically. *Who does that?!* Apparently, our kid. I have empathy for her because she did not have the same amount of time to socialize and experience in-person learning as her sister. She was also only five going on six years old. Most adults cannot sit on a Zoom call that long without wanting to take a picture of their face and call it a day. However, we had to set some expectations. We reminded her to slow down so she could work on her assignments thoroughly and have us review her homework before she submitted it. This generated more questions for us on the homework assignments and exasperated exchanges between her and my husband. However, she did well for the rest of the year.

Hybrid Model

Once the county and school district were in a lower risk category for COVID, the staff decided that they would welcome students back three times a week and continue virtual learning two times a week. The teachers were highly organized, coordinated, and prepared. We signed up for a time slot to meet the kids' teachers with masks on, of course. Each of the teachers had a plastic bucket for each child with all of their materials to kick off the school year, which included books, notebooks, crayons, rulers, etc. The day we met the teachers, I was having extreme stomach pains, including a burning sensation throughout my upper abdomen. I am no stranger to gastritis, as I had a bad bout during college and had to give up on marinara or tomato-based sauces, foods high in citrus, and the occasional drink. I figured I must have eaten a stale burrito because my husband brought it home from lunch after a few days of it being refrigerated.

During the brief meeting with Oz's teacher, I started to sweat, and my stomach felt like it was on fire. I had to get some air, followed by squatting down and then feeling dizzy. I was disappointed and embarrassed that I could not interact with her teacher because she was so positive, enthusiastic, and thorough! I was also so excited for my daughter because if anyone could do this Zoom teaching thing, it seemed like this teacher. Ya Ya came out to sit with me, patting my back and asking me if I was okay. After the meeting ended, Oz's teacher even came out to ask if I needed to use the restroom. I was doubling over in pain as we made our way to Ya Ya's classroom. I smiled weakly as Ya Ya's new teacher handed us her box of supplies and welcomed her to the class. Ya Ya shyly took her box and listened to her new teacher's expectations.

Once the visits were over, I walked to the car hunched over, sweating, and clutching my stomach. When we got home, I immediately went to bed. After several years of emergency room visits and testing, I learned that these were flair-ups likely due to Irritable Bowel Syndrome (IBS). I use the term *likely* because IBS is a diagnosis typically given by excluding other gastrointestinal disorders. Whatever the diagnosis, the treatment includes lifestyle and diet changes, such as coping with the worry that you will need to be in close proximity to a toilet. *Fun times!*

Tech Problems

There was a cultural shift for many of us who used technology for work, school, or socialization. Routine exchanges included telling your coworkers, "I can't hear you. You're on mute." Many times, I had to manage my frustration with those who struggled with the tech. I am a firm believer in karma, and likely due to this frustration, we experienced problems when Oz needed to take a state test at the end of the year. My husband was in the office for a day-long meeting with various colleagues/sites in the area so it was a rare instance when he could not bring the kids to work for Zoom school. It was also the first day of the state-wide exams for third, fourth, and fifth graders. I was not particularly worried about the testing because my husband downloaded the secure browser on Oz's computer the previous day.

But while I was sleeping, Ya Ya ran into my bedroom, "Mommy, what's the password to the internet? I keep getting kicked out!"

Oz also said her computer was not connecting either and I worried

Cancel the Filter

that she wouldn't be able to take the test. I signed Ya Ya in to ensure that Oz had a secure connection, and I linked her to my phone's hotspot. Phew, the crisis was averted, and I returned to bed. School progressed, and a bit later, I jolted up out of bed because Oz was crying because she couldn't connect and the problem-solving with the teacher and principal was not resolving the issue. I rushed to the screen bare-faced, which is equivalent to me feeling naked. Remember, even when I had my C-section, I had a full face on. I desperately tried to jump-start my brain and tried multiple devices to no avail.

I had no choice but to call in reinforcements; I told my husband this was an emergency. In all fairness, it was an academic emergency, which in my orbit is a lower-tiered one. Luckily, my husband works close by. I was on edge which put him on edge. He tried to use Oz's computer, and it did not work. He then downloaded the browser on his computer, and they were able to gain access. After work, he realized on the browser in the advanced settings, that you must select, "don't run apps in the background." Something I wished I knew while checking the task manager on two computers! *Well, f*ck! You don't know what you don't know.*

On a side note, Oz's teacher was amazing because she knew our child inherited/absorbed my anxiety and she said, "Oz, in the larger scheme of things, this is nothing."

When Oz was able to get back on the computer, she finished the exam in thirty minutes. It was more stressful to get on the secure browser than to finish the exam. Oh, virtual school!

After lunch, my husband rushed back during his lunch break to take the girls to the in-person portion of the now, hybrid model. Two weeks into returning to school, they were quite happy to see people again. However, this left parents who were fortunate to work remotely in a tough spot. By the time I ate lunch and worked some more, it was time to pick them up. It was also a surreal process. If I were an anthropologist like Enoch in *Agents of S.H.I.E.L.D.,* I would observe adults in masks, lining up with signs to be read by staff on a bullhorn, alerting our kids that their caregivers were here to pick them up. There was also the option of sitting in your car with the sign on your dashboard. But I had received a pro tip from my husband: Park the car and wait in line. It was a lot quicker! Then, we returned home, and everyone resumed work.

That day reinforced that my husband and I operate as a team. What one is unable to do, the other will pick up the slack. This was a stressful time and still uncharted territory, hybrid schooling, and then taking a state exam at home with a secure browser to reduce the risk of kids cheating—it was a lot. Oz wouldn't even think to cheat off someone else or need to, but we live in an age where you can Google pretty much everything. Fast forward to 2023: AI makes Google look like the old DOS.

In the Blink of an Eye

Literal tech issues were not the only challenge that arose from virtual classes. Many children were in need of glasses at earlier ages than pre-COVID. Following a year of virtual class, Ya Ya developed rapid eye blinking. When we emailed the pediatrician, he deemed it as a tic, which typically resolves itself on its own. My husband took her to see the optometrist who instead of noting that she had never examined a child younger than eight years old, proceeded with the exam, but could not get an accurate reading. In all fairness, asking a six year old to complete an eye exam is very challenging.

After returning to in-person learning, it seemed the tic resolved itself. However, after a quarter of the year had passed, it reappeared, and the blinking was very rapid. We were unsure if it was stress, feeling tired, and/or poor eyesight. We took her to another optometrist who had experience examining children, and she noted that she saw more children with eye problems due to virtual learning. She patiently conducted the exam, despite inconsistent responses from Ya Ya. As a result, she even dilated her eyes to get a more accurate reading of her eyesight. There was a large discrepancy between the initial reading and following dilation—negative six to a barely-there prescription. She stated that this may be a case of over-accommodated vision and Ya Ya had been compensating for her vision issues so well. The optometrist recommended we get glasses to see if the brain-eye connection could assist her in resolving the rapid blinking. Thankfully, her blinking began to significantly decrease and

Cancel the Filter

she was no longer in need of glasses the following year! I encourage parents to advocate for their children when seeing healthcare professionals and identify ones that have the expertise needed for the given situation. This goes for yourselves as well!

A Return to In-Person Learning

The kids returned to in-person school full-time in Fall 2021, and while many parents, including us, experienced worry over COVID-19, most of us really wanted our kids to return to playing with each other, learning from their teachers without being separated by a technological screen, and honestly, having a brief window of silence in the house. Teacher assignments were sent out to the parents, and Oz was shocked to see an unfamiliar name. My husband and I did the routine of texting all the parents we are close to, wondering if our children were in the same class. Ya Ya got the teacher she wanted because Oz had the teacher previously, but a friend who she had been with since kindergarten was in a different class. She began bawling and I stood there shocked! She was typically not one to cry about class assignments, but upon further discussion, she wailed, "I lost [friend]!"

"Honey, you didn't lose her. You can still play with her during recess."

"I lost her!"

I suppose at this developmental age, she could not quite process this concept and this friend was a secure base for her. We continued to assure her that the friendship was not lost, and that this situation would provide her with a new opportunity to make friends.

My husband and I joined the girls on their first day of school. The girls were so happy to see their friends again. A lot had changed since last school year with masks always worn, hand sanitizer stations everywhere around the school, and parents not being able to walk freely around campus after checking in with the administrative office. There were also multiple entry points assigned based on your child's grade level. It was a bit chaotic and there was a lot of wandering around. The crossing guard, commonly referred to as Superman, was fielding questions by kindly stating, "I'm just the janitor." Translation: "This is above my pay grade." It was reminiscent of my colleague and close friend who recently retired.

When the girls returned home from school, they were ecstatic. Oz thought her teacher was so cool because he had a black belt in karate and played percussion in a band. I was impressed that he got a master's from UC Berkeley. Ya Ya was still warming up to returning to school, but I could tell she was very happy.

Parent-Teacher Conference

We were Ya Ya's teacher's first parent-teacher conference this year via Zoom, and the teacher felt comforted that it was with a family who she was already accustomed to. She happily reported that Ya Ya was reading at a grade level above her current grade and was a math whiz—her words! Her vocabulary was also advanced. Ya Ya was described as kind and empathic, and willing to help her classmates. Her teacher recommended that she slow down as she often speeds through her work and does what is minimally required. I laughed because that is Ya Ya. She likely reads the fastest out of the whole family, and apparently, the teacher said she comprehends everything based on test results. Before receiving this feedback, I thought Ya Ya was playing us by pretending to read. My heart felt so full, and I felt so much pride hearing the report, although I was not surprised. In contrast, my husband appeared shocked that she was so advanced. After the call, I did the "I told you so."

Oz's teacher, on the other hand, had a monotone voice and was at a slower pace than I prefer, but it helped *me* to slow down. We were happy and full of pride that Oz was reading two academic years above her grade level, and her assessment in math was a sixty-six out of fifty-seven, which she took great pride in! Oz started off strong in her writing abilities and continued to work on structuring paragraphs. While I was a bit disappointed that there would not be formal Asian American studies

Cancel the Filter

taught, the teacher explained that it was difficult to add content because there is a pressure to "teach the curriculum," and social studies is not taught every day. However, he encouraged us to enroll Oz and her sister in jiu-jitsu, especially since karate taught him discipline and goal setting. Funny enough, during the conference, Oz walked by and waved at her teacher. She must've known we were talking about her, and she later confirmed she saw us on his screen.

My husband later relayed the feedback to the girls after school. I reinforced how proud I was of them, "Ya Ya, your teacher said you are kind and helpful."

"I am?" She tilted her head back. "Just not here [at home]."

"Why not?" I asked.

"I can be vicious and crazy," she replied.

There goes that advanced vocabulary and emotional intelligence.

Oz stated that she was not surprised, anticipating "getting all A's."

"Honey, there are no grades given yet," I chuckled.

The conferences were a win for all of us after all these months of stress. It also reinforced the effectiveness of Kumon and all our hard work together.

<u>Drama</u>

Ya Ya came home distraught, and said, "Mommy, I had the worst day."

"What happened, baby?" I asked.

"Lisa said I put up an 'L' for loser to her friend, but I didn't! She kept saying that and wouldn't play with me," she cried.

"Maybe you could explain it to her tomorrow."

"I tried, but she kept saying I did it," she cried.

"You can try again tomorrow."

* * *

The next day, Ya Ya reported that she cried at school. "I tried to tell Lisa that I didn't do it, and someone said it was the other Ya Ya but she wouldn't believe it."

I tried to make sense of what she was saying. Seven-year-olds are not always reliable reporters, but I also wanted to ask open-ended questions and validate her concerns. Since I had Lisa's mother's phone number, I texted her because I wanted to understand why Ya Ya's best friend was responding to her in this way. If Ya Ya had performed hurtful behavior, I also wanted to know, and of course, correct the behavior.

"Oh my gosh! Lisa was just telling me about this," Lisa's mother said.

"Would the girls be able to have a call with us in the background?" I asked.

Both girls had to bathe and eat dinner so we agreed to have them chat after they finished their routines. I waited for over an hour for the text, despite it being my turn to take a shower. Of course, when I was halfway out of the shower, they were available. I nudged my husband to stand behind Ya Ya. He looked at me with puzzlement because he did not know why he needed to be present for the call. I gritted my teeth and told him that I wanted him to observe their behaviors.

He told me Lisa's parents asked Ya Ya about the situation, and Ya Ya kindly told them her side of the story. She internalized my coaching to state the facts as she saw them, and not focus on who was right or wrong. Instead, she told Lisa that she wanted to continue being best friends, to play with her and make things better. Throughout most of the conversation, Lisa was silent. Her parents said that she had to warm up, and they eventually played via FaceTime.

* * *

The following week, Ya Ya came home again, looking sad and defeated. "Lisa says she hates me a little."

"Huh? What happened?"

"She was playing with one of our friends and kept running away. When I tried to play with them, she ignored me. I asked her, "Do you hate me?" She said, "A little.""

Cancel the Filter

By this time, my patient husband said, "I told her to stop being friends with her. Something must be going on with Lisa."

I asked more open-ended questions and explained to Ya Ya that sometimes we have to make choices as to who to be friends with, and if someone is going to be repeatedly rude to you, it may not be a good idea to spend time with them.

"I don't want to lose her," she cried.

"I understand, honey, but I wouldn't want to be friends with someone who wasn't treating me nicely," I soothed.

Wow, Mean Girls, Elementary School Edition.

Fundraising

My husband and I are both products of the public school system, and we both turned out relatively fine. As a result, I have always been a firm believer in free information and education. Plus, we already paid for preschool, and will more than likely have to pay for college, and, if they want to go, graduate school; that is the the tax of being middle class. Despite not sending the girls to private school, here is a warning to parents with younger children: Don't get it twisted. Schools have been historically underfunded, especially public schools, so there will be non-stop requests for donations. The beginning of the school year is packed with requests for contributions for lunches for the teachers during conference week, walk-a-thons, holiday chocolates, etc. The walk-a-thon is special for the kids because there are tiers of prizes for students based on the amount raised. The popular prizes are a students versus teachers kickball competition and an opportunity to dunk the principal in a water tank.

On a side yet related note, in college, my part-time job was fundraising for my school. Every university has an outreach and development program where requests are made to alumni, parents, and stakeholders to make monetary contributions to the school. Ever notice that campus buildings have individual or family names on them? They paid a pretty penny. Overall, I absolutely loved my job because I met my closest friends there whom I still maintain contact with to this day. In hindsight, that job taught me to not be afraid of making requests of others. Once you've asked many people for thousands of dollars, you are not afraid of asking most people for things. Did I get hung up on or rudely spoken to? Absolutely, but I also had great conversations and made a difference, raising $250,000 over four years!

I had a lightbulb moment. Oz was now old enough to have a spiel or pitch for these donations. Like in my college days (Wow, I sound old), I helped her script an ask and practice it to sound natural. We rarely went out during the pandemic, but my first cousin and his wife were pregnant, and we were going to the baby shower at a restaurant. The script read as follows:

Would you please contribute to SCHOOL's Walk-a-Thon? We are raising money for computers and school supplies. We would really appreciate it and I'm trying to reach my first goal of $100. [When a child raises this amount, they get a walk-a-thon t-shirt]. *Could you help?*

Oz had already practiced the script a few times with her grandparents, and I coached her not to get in my father's face, saying, "Please, please, please" until he donated.

Also, "Let Grandma take off her shoes when she comes home before cornering her," I told her.

Oz loves to bake and made gooey chocolate chip cookies with and without walnuts for the baby shower. Although she didn't intend for the cookies to be a bribe, the timing worked out perfectly. She passed out her famous, around our house, cookies to all the attendees. I suggested that she make her ask after everyone had dinner. I also made a game-time decision to only ask our immediate family because there wasn't time to build rapport with everyone in attendance, and I didn't want to look tacky. I reinforced the purpose of the exercise to my family members. "It's not about the money [*it really wasn't*]. It is about her not being afraid to talk to people."

My relatives were good sports. Oz successfully raised enough money to reach her second goal of $150, giving her a ticket for the school's raffle. But Ya Ya had not received her envelope for the fundraiser and was less than enthusiastic to practice her pitch. In fact, she was downright grumpy and didn't ask any of my relatives. By the next Monday, she got

Cancel the Filter

her envelope, and she had all her money from her wallet in two fistfuls. My husband firmly told her that she could donate after she asked others. She had already collected a dollar from an afterschool provider and ten dollars from her friend. My husband was upset and told her to return the ten dollars, "You can't ask kids. They don't know what they are doing." Ya Ya began to cry in her room, and my husband explained to her that she had to ask adults who could make those decisions.

When Ya Ya went to shower, I told my husband that earning another donation would encourage her to keep fundraising. My husband then told Ya Ya that she could ask Oz after dinner. They both mutually contributed to each other's envelopes and made donations themselves. With Oz and my coaching, Ya Ya got through her pitch, often turning hesitantly toward me for help. A few days later, they went through their pitches with me again. I didn't make it easy. I asked them, "What are you going to use the money for?"

"To fix the lights," Oz sputtered.

"I pay taxes to fix the lights," I replied nonchalantly.

"It's to help buy computers and school supplies," both chimed.

"Okay, how much?"

"Twenty dollars," Oz said.

"Okay. Your turn, Ya Ya."

Ya Ya did her pitch. "How much?" I asked.

"Um, thirty dollars?" she asked, hesitantly.

"Okay."

After the pitches, I gave them feedback to ask higher, but expect less. They listened and appeared satisfied with what they received.

Decisions, Decisions: Vacation or School Event?

My birthday has always been a big deal to me, and oftentimes, I get emo, wondering if I even have any friends who will come to my party. In the past, my parties have always been filled with loved ones, so this fear of rejection is merely an unrealistic fear. Recently, perhaps so I don't have to deal with the fear, coupled with the fact that we have the financial means to do so, I've been going on vacation during my birthday month. Due to the pandemic, we decided to go to Southern California and stay with our friend. However, we did not anticipate having to quarantine five days after returning home and presenting a negative COVID-19 test. Typically, we would have no problem with this, but if the girls missed five days of school, they would not be able to attend the walk-a-thon.

I had already resolved to not go on the trip because I wanted to be the "good" mom and not rob them of the experience with their friends and this childhood milestone. My husband left it up to them though, "Do you want to go on vacation or the walk-a-thon?"

"Vacation," Ya Ya quickly responded.

"I don't know. I want to go on vacation, but I want to go to the walk-a-thon with my friends. I don't want to miss the dunk tank," Oz said, her face filled with anguish. Throughout the night, she paced back and forth with tears in her eyes.

"Honey, you already know what you want to do, but you feel guilty. You don't need to be sorry or feel guilty. I just want you to be happy," I soothed and genuinely meant it. Plus, they had worked hard to fundraise for the event.

"But it's your birthday and you always go to my birthday!" she sobbed.

"It's fine, honey. Daddy and I plan to go there the following month anyway for the BTS concert. I'm going no matter what!"

"What if we meet Rosanna Pansino?"

"Honey, she is not having a meet-and-greet," I said calmly. *This was another one of her FOMO worries.*

"We might see her on the street," she reasoned.

"Southern California is a big place," I countered.

She continued to cry and lament. I kept reassuring her that she did not need to apologize. But Oz made her decision and continued to apologize. When it was lights out, my husband strode over to their bedroom, "Stop apologizing. It's not your fault and you don't need to be sorry. Go to bed," he said, visibly irritated and gritting his teeth.

I turned towards him, "Honey, that's a bit harsh."

Cancel the Filter

"She's apologized fifty times already and we've already told her it's not her fault," he countered.

Again, I soothed everyone and said, "It's fine. There is no need to feel sorry or guilty. Good night."

My husband and I are firm advocates of girls and women not apologizing for everything. Of course, apologize for a legitimate reason, such as hurting someone's feelings, or stepping on someone's toes metaphorically or physically, but unlearn the programming of operating apologetically. After all, there was nothing to apologize for. My husband and I went to Southern California the following month without the kids, connecting with friends and going to a BTS concert, and we had a blast!

Unfortunate Impact of COVID

Despite the positive impact K-pop groups were having on the world, increasing the visibility of Asian talent, Anti-Asian hate crimes skyrocketed in the United States. The Stop Asian Americans and Pacific Islanders (AAPI) Hate reporting centers received close to 4,000 incidents, and these crimes occurred in the context of over 350,000 deaths from COVID by the Centers for Disease Control & Prevention. There appeared to be a correlation between increases in hate crimes and the then-presidential administration's assertion that COVID should be called Kung-Flu because it reportedly originated in China. This left many Asian Americans fearing for their loved ones' safety. In fact, we bought my mother pepper spray and a whistle so she could take it to work. I saw an increase in Asian Americans presenting for therapy in my practice, which saddened me, and also made me hopeful that they were combating the stigma of seeking help. As many Asian Americans began to speak out, communities began to mobilize to address our concerns, no longer resigned to silently suffering a history of racial injustice.

Cancel the Filter on Being a Psychologist

Being an Asian American psychologist has always been significant to my identity because I felt my community needed therapists who look like me. This became even more apparent as Anti-Asian hate crimes significantly increased and Asian Americans sought therapists who could help them through collective and personal traumas. Becoming a mother and traveling have strengthened my ability to build rapport, be empathic, and work with diverse clients in psychotherapy through the lens of cultural humility. While the effectiveness of therapy is not guaranteed by matching therapist-client demographics, it can help in some instances to build rapport and a therapeutic relationship, which may improve client engagement in treatment. Therefore, it has been important to me to include questions about culture, race, and ethnicity in a psychosocial intake, and if clinically relevant, discuss ways that these factors impact a client's presenting concerns. Assuming an integrative and culturally humble stance in therapy translates into applying therapy modalities and techniques that are clinically indicated, and not assuming that you know a person's culture. The client is treated as an expert in their experience.

My approach to treatment has been shaped by my life experiences, formal college education, graduate training, and over a decade of working with diverse clients. It was in graduate school that I truly felt under-represented. While my class was diverse in age, sexual orientation, ethnicity, and religiosity, the staff was not reflective of these diverse demographics. Sometimes I felt like a broken record when we were discussing clients and I asked, "What about culture?"

In addition to challenging the theories and practices established by a historically homogenous group of theorists, I sought practicums and internships where diversity-related factors were integrated into the training and treatment of clients. These training experiences led me to work at a psychiatric hospital in Washington D.C. with specialty programming for clients who identified as LGBTQ+ and were diagnosed with co-occurring mental health issues, and those diagnosed with Substance Use Disorders (SUDs). It was during this training experience that I became interested in working with individuals coping with SUDs and psychosocial issues (homelessness, unemployment, mood disorders, identity development).

My interests led to a specialty in Homeless Rehabilitation and SUD Treatment, allowing me to further examine ways that diversity-related factors intersect with an individual's presenting issues. This included reflecting on my stimulus value as a young, Asian American, female doctor and it took years of training, practice, and ongoing reflection to set boundaries when a client may say something inappropriate (commenting on my looks, ethnicity, or age) to me. Being pregnant during my internship and residency gave me great practice in setting boundaries as to how much I would share about my personal life.

Bring Your Kids to Work

A few years after having children, I was rather unapologetic about having kids and a career. Now, I'm not advocating that everyone takes this approach because many workplaces are either covertly or overtly hostile towards working parents. I have been fortunate to advance my career, in addition to being open about being a parent. Therefore, ever since my children were young, I've tried to include them in important work events. I proudly toted Oz on my left arm as a baby when I accepted my certificate of completion for residency. My supervisor praised me for my work and acknowledged it, particularly while raising a baby!

Shortly after Ya Ya was born, I received an award for mentorship. I strolled Ya Ya to the ceremony on my day off. As I accepted the award, the chief of staff rolled the stroller slowly, back and forth, while Ya Ya stared at him and cried. When Ya Ya could run around, I gave a speech at my graduation for the Leadership Development Institute. She ran around the tables that were filled with guests, including my immediate family.

Before the pandemic and an incident (described below), I have brought my husband and kids to graduations of veterans who have completed treatment programs and maintained sobriety. This gave them perspective on what Mommy does and who they generously split my time with. I would like them to internalize the message to help others. Similarly, Oz has helped at our annual holiday party for veterans, handing out plates to veterans for their meals. She ran up and down the line to ensure everyone got one.

I want to emphasize that I have chosen and continue to create a work environment where family is the priority *and* a welcome part of our lives. As a supervisor, when colleagues tell me that their nanny or their kid missed the bus, I don't think twice about excusing them from work. To accommodate these occurrences, we've cross-trained staff so that we always have coverage. In addition, I have observed that colleagues work hard if they know they have your support. They would probably take care of their personal business anyways (I would) but giving me the courtesy of a heads-up and me acknowledging it, can convey the message I want to promote: *Don't be afraid of negative consequences at work, or me judging you in a negative way for taking care of your family.* I just hope that society continues to evolve to positively support and assist working parents in engaging in meaningful work and raising their children.

Say My Name, Say My Name (Cue the original members of Destiny's Child)

There are many amazing female performers who are so well-known, they only need one name—Aaliyah, Brandy, Madonna, and Beyoncé, to name a few. No one asks them for their middle initial or last name. Sure, we know that Beyoncé's is Knowles. But the point is, no one introduces

Cancel the Filter

her as Beyonce Knowles. Unfortunately, I am not in their company, and my common name has led to many annoying and hilarious mix-ups. Likewise, my husband's name is common, and his inbox is filled with emails from various senders around the world who intended to send them to the 100th person with his name. He's even received a love letter, and yes, I confirmed it was not for him. The receiver later joked, "I missed my opportunity." He's gotten concert tickets, vacation pictures, receipts for purchases, and shared locations—all because of his common name!

I call it the "Chronicles of Being a Stephanie" when I'm relaying the mix-ups to my co-worker. A postdoctoral fellow and I had the same name, and we would often get added as additional signers on notes and oftentimes receive the other's emails. One day, I couldn't get into any of the systems for work and thought I'd typed in my password incorrectly, or simply that the portal wasn't working. Eventually, I ended up contacting the IT help desk and discovered that because the fellow with the same name completed her training and left the hospital, my name was erroneously deleted from the system! I confirmed with the help desk that I had been at the same hospital for nine years at the time.

Later, the same fellow was hired as a psychologist, and it became more obvious that our emails were not being delivered accurately. I was getting her virtual appointment reminders and getting added as an additional signer on patient notes. When the COVID-19 pandemic began to impact operations, a memo was sent to my supervisor, which led him to email me urgent communications. We eventually spoke on the telephone, but I received the referenced email three days later! I also received several emails from a psychologist on the training committee who asked me to present on a topic for the new interns. When the training director returned, she called to apologize that they had meant to ask, "the other Stephanie." She was embarrassed and while the mix-up was understandable, I unfortunately spent time on the presentation and asked staff to compile data for it. I was more apologetic towards them.

My favorite instance was receiving her tentative job offer and being informed that HR would be checking my references. I explained the common mix-up, and that receiving a job offer was a "new one."

Of course, the universe later served me a slice of humble pie. I misspelled a podcast guest's name on a Word document, reminding me that we are all human.

Fear

Fear is an interesting emotion because it is accompanied by physical and psychological components—tension in the body, headaches, anxiety, sweat, and can even manifest as a physical paralysis. The fight-or-flight aspect of our biology is well-documented, and when we are scared, we either engage/react (fight) or we flee (take flight). It was a helpful mechanism back during the days when we were running from bears and snakes. It's not so much anymore as we are faced with overstimulation regularly. That is not to say that it is not helpful now, as there is such a thing as a healthy amount of fear in situations. However, Jim Kwik in his book, *Limitless*, puts fear into perspective by asking himself, *"Is this danger real or imagined?"*

I, along with others, have experienced fear many times in my life. I typically worry about the worst that could happen. *Will I fail this exam* (in my young mind, that was less than an A or A+)? *Would I be able to afford next quarter's tuition at school? Will my daughter be born safely?* In two of the former situations, the fear and worry motivated me to study harder, apply for scholarships, and work a part-time job, but in hindsight, the fear was excessive. The latter situation was a realistic fear due to Oz being born prematurely and her stay in the NICU.

Occupational Hazard

My work as a clinician has led to fear in less than a handful of incidents. After all, I work with a solid, supportive team that values safety, empathy, and patient care. In private practice, there have been a few acute patients, but none of whom I felt jeopardized my safety (knock on wood). However, the incident that led to the most fear was when a client who was not a client of mine, but part of a program I directed—was threatening me through email, fifty-one to be exact.

I had never considered getting a restraining order for myself in over ten years of my career, but this was impacting my family, and I had an overwhelming need to feel protected. I completed the required paperwork, added the email evidence, and presented it to the courthouse, second in line, at 2:00 p.m. The case was reviewed second to last! In this situation, handing it in first placed you on the bottom of the pile. I was called in by the bailiff who directed me to talk to the court researcher. She stated that my paperwork did not clearly document the threat so I had to come back. But then the judge entered.

"You seem to be mistaken as to how this process works. You have a responsibility and a burden to fill out this paperwork correctly," the judge's voice boomed. I have twenty stacks of these on my desk and you expect me to go through all these emails? You can come back tomorrow."

"We've been waiting for two hours," I said, weakly.

"You can come back tomorrow because I have a meeting at 4:00," he said.

I glanced at the clock, and it was 3:55 p.m.

"The paperwork is not filled out correctly. If you don't know how to do it, seek legal advice," he said, curtly.

I tried to explain that we did not know the process.

"I'll tell you what?" said the judge. "Your request is denied."

I could feel the tears well up in my eyes. "They are psychotic," I mumbled. In my mind, I was referring to the client, but the judge heard me and thought I was referring to him.

"*EXCUSE ME?*" he barked.

Of course, clarification was needed: I meant the perpetrator, not the judge. The tears were raining from my eyes. The judge softened for just one second before he told us, again, to fill out the paperwork and come back tomorrow.

When he left the room, the researcher told us how to best proceed with the paperwork.

I started to hyperventilate and sob. I felt so helpless. I had already taken the proper measures to contact the police several times, file police reports, and follow up with a behavioral committee at work. This reminded me of the *Dangerous Minds* scene where Emilio doesn't knock on the principal's door, and he gets sent away. That's the night he gets shot. I hoped that this would be resolved in a very different way for me. Bureaucracy and technicalities can cost lives. To make matters worse, when you feel unprotected, unheard, and unseen, helplessness starts to kick in, and sometimes, this can feel worse than fear.

I want to emphasize the point that this is not a situation where one person's issue should be generalized to all clients seeking treatment. This was the worst situation I have come across in terms of personal safety. But given the current sociopolitical climate, the increase in gun violence, and attacks on Asian Americans, I looked to the legal system to assist us, or at least someone with that professional stature to speak kindly and empathically.

Round Two

I was dreading returning to court the next day. So much so that I avoided re-filling out the paperwork until the very last hour my husband picked me up. The paperwork essentially requires you to relive a trauma, and I did not want to spend any more mental space thinking about it. It was looming though. I was also hoping that it would not take more than two hours for someone to read the paperwork this time.

Fortunately, there were only three other people in line that day. We returned to the same cast of characters. But this time I told the bailiff that he was kind and it seemed like he genuinely wanted to help others. I then suggested that there be paralegals to answer questions about paperwork and he inquired about whether the law library had such assistance. The response was that there were some paralegals, but they were sitting in another building, and likely did not see many people.

The judge never appeared to see us face-to-face. However, the court researcher returned with the granted orders of no contact, harassment, or being within 100 yards of me. Once you receive this paperwork, you go to the clerk's office on the first floor to schedule a court date and

Cancel the Filter

obtain the required signatures and stamps. You then go to the third floor to the sheriff's department and request they serve the paperwork to the "restrained." This is a free service because theoretically, the "protected" doesn't want to endanger their lives by serving the "restrained" in person. You then drive to the local police station and give them a copy of the restraining order.

I later called the sheriff's department to check on the status of whether the restrained was served, and the person was not served. Follow-up calls also revealed that the restrained was not answering the door and was not served. If the restrained is not served the paperwork, the restraining order is *not* in effect. If not served within five days of the court hearing, you need to request an extension of the court date, and yes, the burden is on the victim.

* * *

Upon contacting the clerk's office to inquire if additional paperwork needed to be completed to request an extension of the court date, they stated that all I needed was to indicate that I would like an extension and that no additional paperwork was needed. This was "sus" in a highly bureaucratic system, but I followed what was told to me. On this day, the judge was a different one from the initial meetings. I pressed the button to go up the elevator, and the up button was notably upside down. The elevator brought us to the dimly lit, fourth floor where on a column someone wrote that "Lil _____ was a rat, a rat-ta-tat-tat." I submitted the documents when the bailiff opened the door.

The bailiff then called everyone into the courtroom and who do we see? The court recorder with an awful attitude. She proceeded to raise her voice with an irritated tone, "Who is Stephanie? Everyone else needs to leave."

We were all confused since the bailiff had summoned us to go inside the courtroom.

"You don't have your required paperwork so I can't present the extension to the judge," she said with irritation.

"I called the clerk's office and they said we didn't need any additional paperwork."

"I don't know why they would tell you that because you need paperwork," she said.

"If we go downstairs, can we fill it out and come back?" I asked.

"You can try, and I can ask the judge, but there is no guarantee she will review it," she said.

I rushed to the elevator and called the number on the clerk's office door. They continued to express confusion over the required paperwork. They finally found the forms and it was a scramble to fill them out on the elevator and then, on the bench. There was one question, "Is a restraining order in effect?" I checked "Don't Know" because although there was one, it technically was never served. We submitted the paperwork to the bailiff and waited, last in line.

When called into the courtroom, the researcher made it a point to say, "You were missing some information, but the judge filled it in for you. You also didn't have a copy of the original restraining orders, so we made copies."

"We have a copy," I said, seething.

"Oh, well you didn't give it to us."

The researcher reviewed the extension and directed me to go to the clerk's office to schedule a court date and get the required signatures and stamps. It is notable that the information missing was whether the restraining order was in effect.

Back down to the clerk's office, I called the number on the door and a different clerk worked on our paperwork.

I reviewed the paperwork. "Where's the new court date?" I asked.

The clerk looked puzzled and recognition appeared on his face, registering the missing information.

Then, back up to the third floor to the sheriff's department. Thank the Buddha for the one employee who was thorough and friendly. She immediately observed that the clerk's office did not stamp the courthouse's address on my documents.

"Jesus Christ, another mistake," I said, exasperated, as I proceeded to take the elevator back downstairs. I called the number, and the clerk took the paperwork and retreated to stamp the documents.

"Here you go. Problem solved."

Excuse me, the clerk caused the problem, I thought.

Cancel the Filter

Back upstairs. The sheriff's department staff member went line by line through the paperwork, noting errors that I corrected on the spot. I was so impressed by her attention to detail, and it was refreshing after a long day of being told I did not do X, Y, and Z and having to correct mistake after mistake by the clerk's office. Now that there was someone who was meticulous and friendly, I asked about the process of serving the restrained. Notably, the detectives are the ones who attempt to serve the restrained and they dress in suits. However, they often knock on the door and identify themselves with the sheriff's department. They then leave their business card if the restrained does not open the door.

They are not going to open their fuckin' door if they see and hear that, I thought.

I left the courthouse feeling deflated. When I got into the car, I just screamed, releasing the frustration I had stifled for the past two hours. I soon began ranting and cussing up a storm. As if I needed another reason, I completely lost faith in the justice system that day. I felt like I was treated like a piece of shit. I can reason now that the researcher might have started in her job as a reasonable, understanding person, and was hardened over the years. But it still didn't assuage me from feeling like another piece of paper to her.

Terror

The situation with this individual left me feeling anxious about opening my work emails and receiving any inkling that I was on this person's radar. I eventually received the package at the hospital indicating that the sheriff made two attempts to serve the person the initial restraining order. Unfortunately, it got worse. I was alerted to a Google review of my private practice that attacked my ethics and morals as a hospital provider and a person. Now, this behavior was no longer restricted to a hospital where most practitioners would know to evaluate the context, but my business. My business is like my third child, and I felt helpless that I could not protect my child. I began to feel intense fear spread throughout my body. I called for my husband with panic in my voice, and the kids picked up on this panic. My husband and I went into the home office, and I showed him the review. It felt like I was being punched over and over because now this person was creeping into all aspects of my life.

My husband was level-headed and researched how to flag the review as inappropriate. It was just a quick click on three dots in the upper right-hand corner. To make matters even more stressful, despite submitting a report, it would take three days to receive a response from Google. My husband looked at me in disbelief as I began to sob, telling him how devastated I was. While I was beyond criticism on graduate school papers, this was an attack on my reputation, which severely hurt me because I practiced with integrity and empathy.

I contacted my three colleagues who all listened with empathy and compassion and were also frustrated. Two suggested that they contact the person together to assess what the person was hoping to accomplish. The other colleague advised me to sue for defamation and print out the review immediately. I agreed with all recommendations, and I strongly gravitated towards the aspect of the situation that I could control—consulting with a lawyer to protect myself and my family.

Legal Representation

I felt fortunate to have friends refer me to a law firm immediately. The intake coordinator picked up and acknowledged the panic and pain in my voice. She listened empathically and attentively, as I verbally vomited all that had occurred over the past several months. Typically, the law firm schedules an intake, but she kindly took down the details and explained the process. First, I would have to pay a retainer of thousands of dollars, and then she would assign a lawyer to my case.

"Okay," I said, feebly, while I silently wanted to pass out at the cost. I told her that I'd talk it over with my husband, although I knew I would proceed. She would draft the paperwork and I thanked her, feeling comforted for the first time in weeks.

That day, I signed all the paperwork and submitted the payment. I

Cancel the Filter

spent four-to-five hours uploading every video message, email, and text that the person sent me, and screenshots of the Google reviews. After the lawyer was assigned to the case, I waited for the strategy session to be scheduled. We then coordinated a time, which wasn't soon enough. I expressed my distress and disappointment that we couldn't meet sooner, as I had only a few days left to serve the person. After getting past the disappointment, she suggested I hire a process server as the restrained was possibly moving between different locations. I agreed and contacted the referral.

* * *

"XYZ Legal Services," Harry (name changed) answered.

I explained the situation, and he stated, "Well, we would have to do a stakeout."

"Okay," I said, again, feebly. "What are the fees?"

"I'll send you the fees to your email. Also, send us your restraining orders and a picture of the restrained."

I did so immediately after hanging up and then almost passed out because it would cost $800 upfront to serve the same individual the two restraining orders and $150/hour for a stakeout, minimum of three hours!

I called my husband immediately, and he contacted XYZ, asking if there was a guarantee that they would serve the individual. There was none. They also wanted me to give them a good window of time to sit outside of the apartment, which I could not provide.

I then contacted the lawyer who was shocked at the cost. I was feeling dread in my stomach that I would have to return to the place that sucks the life out of you— the county courthouse. Fortunately, the lawyer stated she could file a continuance on my behalf.

* * *

A Stakeout

After tossing and turning every night, I began reading articles on the harassment of mental health providers by patients. While I had been viewing the situation through the lens of a psychologist, after reading these articles, it dawned on me that I was being cyberstalked. The stalker was doing such things as going on my podcast's social media page and copying an image and pasting it on my Google Review page. He would also create email accounts with my and my colleague's names within the username. They created a fictitious name for my co-worker with her picture from social media and wrote an awful review that he posted as her on my Google page. The vast landscape of the internet has both benefits and challenges, as the ease with which we can obtain information and connect with others has its pros and cons.

By this time, I had anxiety checking my email, wondering if there would be another picture, review, or threatening email. My lawyer could not obtain any additional information about the continuance request and offered to go to my court date to request the continuance. I told her that I would try to request it the day before the court date, which would save time and money. At the courtroom, I was relieved to see a different recorder who was already significantly kinder and more helpful than the one I saw on all the previous visits. He explained the documents needed and sat with me to ensure that I understood. When he returned with the paperwork, there were a few checkboxes. He was apologetic because the judge recommended coming back on the court date "so as not to confuse the clerks." He nervously stated, "You'll get what you want, but you have to come back tomorrow." *He even knows this is ridiculous.* The energy in my body drained in defeat because there was nothing to be done today.

I contacted my lawyer to let her know the outcome of that day's efforts. She stated, "I would love to go to court with you tomorrow to get the signatures."

What? Why would she need to go to court with me to obtain something that would more than likely occur? I would have to pay for her travel costs and her time by the hour.

Cancel the Filter

"No, I think I'll be fine," I responded politely, and the next day, I obtained the signatures for an extended court date.

* * *

Finally, a porter served the stalker, and I immediately went back to the courthouse to file the proof of service. We called the clerk from outside, and he directed us to a drop-box. It felt anti-climactic, and we took a video of me putting the proof of service in the box, as evidence it was submitted.

* * *

Court Hearing Number One

The day arrived and I was hoping and praying that the defendant would not appear in court. As predicted, the defendant presented to the courthouse using a walker and accompanied by a parent. I began to feel anxiety, fear, and anticipation. I wanted to put the whole situation behind me. My lawyer brought a box full of exhibits—ninety-six pages. My knees buckled as I proceeded into the courtroom after being told to initially wait outside to see how the trial proceeded.

"Raise your right hand," instructed the recorder.

The defendant's parent expressed confusion as to whether they should raise their hand, despite being present as a witness to testify, for what I was not sure. I recalled that their parent called the police on them several times for erratic behavior.

The three of us raised our right hand and swore, "To tell the whole truth and nothing but the truth."

The judge asked the defendant if they had reviewed the brief, expressing surprise that it was ninety-six pages. The defendant noted that he did not review it.

"The brief was sent to the defendant's mailing address," my lawyer said.

"Defendant, do you want time to review the brief?" asked the judge.

They, of course, stated that they would need time, citing mental health issues. The defendant claimed that their lawyer was supposed to submit paperwork to the court. The judge noted that he did not receive anything. The defendant then said that they were unsure if the non-profit lawyer would represent them—a contradiction. The protection orders were resumed until the next court date and no service was needed because the defendant was present. They would now not be able to claim that they did not receive any paperwork.

"Your honor, the brief mostly includes exhibits, and emails sent by the defendant to Dr. Wong. Could they review it and we can come back later in the afternoon?" asked my lawyer.

"I can't expect the defendant to review ninety-six pages in a few hours. We will have to schedule another date."

My stomach dropped and my legs remained weak. The hearing was pushed back for a month. *A whole month*, days before Thanksgiving. All I could think was, *please don't be during the BTS concert*.

When I exited the courtroom, I sat on the bench outside and began to cry in disbelief as I wondered why this person would not agree to leave me alone. My mind raced as sadness and disappointment turned to frustration. The stress just felt insurmountable.

Court Hearing Number Two

I was more hopeful this time because the defendant had been given more than ample time to review the brief, the majority of which they penned themself. My lawyer was also well-prepared with her box of documents and informed the judge that we were ready to proceed. The defendant was then asked if they were prepared to proceed.

"I'm requesting more time, your honor," the defendant said. They spouted some BS about working with a lawyer to represent them, and they only had to give him a check. The judge asked the name of the lawyer.

"I have it right here on my phone," they said.

The entire courtroom waited as they spent the next ten minutes scrolling through their phone with the defendant stating that the lawyer was well known because he had been on television. Eventually, the law firm was named. Yet despite the judge repeatedly asking for a name, the defendant could not provide one, even after we took a fifteen-minute recess!

I prayed that the judge would proceed with the case. I expressed my fears, given the defendant posted an excerpt of the trial brief on social media, and recorded the volunteer in our program without his consent. My stomach dropped as the judge said he would grant another continuance, but if the defendant contacted me directly or indirectly, they would leave the courtroom with "new jewelry," aka handcuffs, with the bailiff. The defendant successfully wasted all our time and another $1500.

D-Day

After the final continuance, the defendant and parent presented to the court, and notably, without legal representation. The judge asked for an estimated timeframe for the hearing, and my lawyer estimated an hour and a half.

"You really think it will take that long?" the judge asked with surprise in his voice. My lawyer did not know what the defendant would present so she stated it could take less time, but to be safe, one and a half hours.

To our surprise, the judge assigned us to another judge and courtroom. The new judge then spent fifteen to twenty minutes reviewing all the documents. So, after all this time and the judge being firm with the defendant the previous session, we were getting a brand-new judge!

When we re-entered the courtroom, the defendant did an about-face and pleaded the fifth. My lawyer then proceeded to implement full questioning so that I could testify. Despite pleading the fifth and swearing that the testimony was "the truth and nothing but the truth," the defendant presented irrelevant information.

Ruling

The new judge was very fair, given the information she was presented with. However, she did not get to see the defendant's behaviors before we appeared in her courtroom. She granted a three-year restraining order with no direct or indirect contact, including no social media postings. She told the defendant that she "deserves to live her life, and you need to stop." She also displayed empathy towards the defendant and stated that they were misdirecting their anger—they needed to focus on his health.

After leaving the courtroom, I felt relief flood over me. At least there was some resolution! On the way back to the car, I started to experience chest and stomach burning, and all the stress just seemed to hit me all at once.

The next day, after taking time to reflect on all the happenings during the past four months, I became very frustrated and upset that the defendant got to walk away without any consequences. The legal system continues to be disappointing all around, particularly since there were violations of the restraining order hours after the judge's decision. I had to cope with the impact on my emotions and mental health. I took comfort in the fact that I used my voice to stand up for my family, myself, and my colleagues by proxy.

Cancel the Filter on Podcasting

The Birth of a Podcast: Color of Success

When I began learning about podcasting, I did not have the grand purpose of using my voice to advocate for mental health in ethnic minority communities. It really started because I *love* free stuff, especially *quality* free stuff. One such instance occurred when Dr. Melvin Varghese offered a free master class on podcasting. Dr. Varghese will always have a special place in my heart because when I was starting my private practice in 2016, I turned to his podcast, "Selling the Couch," to establish and build it. He interviewed guests on how to write copy for a professional website to increase referrals and built a community where colleagues could support each other on their journey. I had no intention of becoming a professional podcaster or using the podcast as a marketing tool because fortunately in 2020, I had a full private practice. I anticipated the class to be solely a learning experience, but it started a whole new chapter in my life.

At around the same time, an Asian community was established on social media, and as I saw inspiring story after another, I also saw the need to discuss mental health among high-achieving and ambitious members. The risk of burnout and mental health issues accompanies working and advancing many of our careers. Seeing this need and topic of interest, I purchased the start-up equipment that Dr. Varghese suggested, the Audio-Technica ATR2100-USB and mic stand to attach to my desk, an audio recording platform, editing software, and a hosting platform. I asked myself, *Why do I want to do this?* I realized I have something special to share because mental health *is* important, and people of color are successful and under-represented. Let us not be ignored! I proposed the idea to the social media community co-founders and asked them to be my first guests. They agreed, and it became real.

Did I say that I like free stuff? Well, I did not want to pay for music for the podcast because I like starting ventures in low-risk situations. For instance, if I decided to do the project after the first episode, we would not be out tons of money. So, I went homemade. My daughters and I had recorded a jingle that we came up with during a vacation to Cabo and I taught myself to edit with free software. I subsequently reached out to a good friend and artist famed for his What If posters to create a logo; check out Peter Stults's episode in the first season. I messaged him a mock-up of a very rudimentary version I made using an art app, and what he turned it into in less than twenty-four hours was beyond any expectations I had. The logo of a pineapple wearing a crown complemented the title, "Color of Success," with the pineapple symbolizing diversity and being welcoming, and the crown communicating success.

I spent the next few weeks recording content for new episodes. My husband read online that you should have three recorded episodes and release them at once so listeners could have content to listen to after the first episode. I followed Dr. Varghese's instructions to publish the episodes, learning how to locate an RSS feed and add it to podcast catalogs. I didn't know it then, but publishing an episode is a feat because the process entails so much more than just recording the discussion.

Social media is an additional beast to tackle. I never paid attention or cared about the number of followers I had on Instagram, and at that point, it was around 300 friends. However, I recognized that I would need to build a following to promote the podcast. *Where do I even start to build a social media presence?* Fortunately, the online Asian community had postings on specific days where members could share their social media accounts to connect with others, and this was one way that I began to network. While it was a follow-for-follow situation, I made sure that I DM'd people to establish a connection, asking them how they were doing during the pandemic, and being curious about their careers, interests, and endeavors. Through this approach, I have met some fantastic people and formed more genuine connections.

A caveat is that not everyone has good intentions. A pet peeve of mine is when someone mutually follows you, only to later unfollow

Cancel the Filter

you. Following a person or business page is supporting someone's journey, that's why it seems inconsiderate to accept someone's support, and then withdraw it. People likely have different views on this, but the behavior is not consistent with my values because I like to surround myself with truly supportive people. There are always exceptions to rules, but one of my rules of thumb: If you see someone with thousands of followers and only following five to ten, it is very unlikely that they will be supporting your page.

As a podcaster and entrepreneur, you are a one-woman team, or so I thought. I was never formally trained in business, but through building a private practice, I had the foundational skills to start a new endeavor. It was and is hard not to become overwhelmed because your attention is pulled in 100 different directions. Recording the content is one of the easiest aspects for me because I was clinically trained to interview people and ask questions using the Socratic method, and to actively listen. Active listening is not just hearing their words, but observing underlying meaning and making connections between themes. My interview style is semi-structured and focuses on truly getting to know a person and their story. While I have questions that integrate the importance of mental health, as famed interviewer Eric Nam says, "I just want to make the guest feel comfortable." Storytelling is both a method and an art form and to do people's stories justice, people need to hear them. I have maintained my public response of, "Do not focus on the number of downloads and views," but let's be honest, no podcaster ignores these metrics completely. In fact, looking at the numbers may respectively lead to joy and despair that someone is listening, but perhaps not as many as you hoped.

There are several times I have wanted to quit the podcasting game, but there have been signs to not give up. One such sign came in the form of a social media post on the group with thousands of Asian members. Someone posted (paraphrased), "Asian males, where do you go to seek help for mental health?" Responses varied, such as "Grab a beer," or "Hug your family." One of my favorites was "Smoke a blunt" or "Don't think about it. Think positively." These may work for some, but if someone is hearing voices, it is difficult to utilize these methods and there was a theme of toxic masculinity in these responses. This post brought me back to *why* I dedicate my energy to destigmatizing mental healthcare in Asian and Asian American communities. Seeking help is *not* a weakness and it is important to normalize asking for help and making an appointment to see a licensed mental health provider.

When I began the podcast, friends, and contacts were my first guests. I am proud that my guests have discussed important topics such as working remotely around the world, moving to another country to broaden their experiences for a job that is consistent with their values, pursuing art despite being discouraged by some, seeking treatment for obsessive-compulsive disorder, coping with burnout, and co-parenting. All of these stories have a common thread— addressing mental health throughout your life and career is essential to success because we all face challenges and self-doubt. Success is relative, but all the guests emphasized finding meaning in your life and work. I have interviewed celebrities who by societal standards are successful, amassing millions of followers, views of their work, and a level of wealth and status many of us don't have. But there has not been one guest who has equated money or views with success. Rather, some have described the pressure of being in the spotlight and how your platform and actions are judged under a microscope. Being able to cope with attention and coinciding criticism requires the implementation of effective coping skills, including fostering self-love.

Many people say that success is a combination of hard work and luck, and I would agree. Early on, as I was contacting people in the group, some members of the group also requested to be on the show, including William Hung who replicated his infamous performance on American Idol of Ricky Martin's "She Bangs." William has embodied strength, perseverance, and the ability to adapt. He pivoted several times in his career, realizing that fame is fleeting, and connecting with others and following new areas of interest are ways to enrich our lives. Chase Tang, an Asian-Canadian actor, and mental health advocate also wanted to collaborate, demonstrating his pure heart, kindness, compassion, and drive. He understands that working in a job that sucks your soul is not mentally healthy, and taking a risk to follow your dreams and give back to others can lead to mental and physical dividends.

But midway through the first season, I recognized that it was a strain

Cancel the Filter

on my husband to edit the shows in his non-existent free time, particularly since he was doing this for me, and I needed help. *Who would feel sorry for me?* I reached out to a childhood friend who was a professional audio/video editor as a side hustle, and someone who has a pure heart just like my husband. We were not generating any income at this point, and my private practice was funding the podcast, therefore, it did not seem financially sound to hire a random person regardless of their talent. My friend said, "Yes," and demonstrated his pure heart, leaving the amount for payment up to me. He joked, "This is why I'm poor."

Of course, I could not pay a corporate-level fee, but I compensated him way above what he was willing to accept. My best friend was also unemployed at the time and was experiencing depression and anxiety. I thought that if I could give her some sense of purpose again by working on a meaningful project, it would motivate her to put herself out there again. She would go on to help with marketing, producing our images for social media and the episode postings, in addition to helping with social notes and miscellaneous tasks. The artist/friend who helped with the logo was also always willing to help anytime we needed something. We now had a small and mighty team and the quality of work that we were able to release into the world improved exponentially! While I loved earlier episodes with our homemade theme song, it was much more polished to have a professionally produced song. I was proud that we recorded and released twenty episodes during the first season, and over 100 episodes to date.

Celebrity culture has always intrigued and interested me, perhaps it has something to do with my achievement-oriented approach to life. Throughout my existence, I've had this frame of reference that being a celebrity equates to being wealthy, beautiful, and admired for your accomplishments. Celebrities stood out from the masses and were remembered for what they accomplished in their lives. As I became an adult, and more celebrities began to disclose details of their personal lives, willingly, or through paparazzi coverage, it became apparent that there was a high price to pay for fame—lack of privacy, criticism, cyber and in-person bullies, mental health challenges, and substance abuse issues. The funny thing is, throughout my life, until it occurred, I never thought I would own a house in the Bay Area or ever achieve a six-figure salary. Regardless of the pros and cons, my fascination persisted, which led to conflicting feelings. The podcast has been a medium to connect with many celebrities in the Asian community, and I have learned about their struggles and triumphs. It has not led me to feel more important or to significantly change my day-to-day life, but rather, I now have first-hand experiences that at the end of the day, they are people just like you and me.

One of the interviews was with Guy Tang who shot to fame for being a hair guru and being his multidimensional self as a musician and reality TV star. During my chat with him, he talked about growing up in Oklahoma and facing racism from White individuals, and not feeling like he belonged among Asian Americans either. What I and so many love about him is his willingness to be vulnerable and honest, in addition to actively responding to people on his social media networks. He did not hold back during the interview either, calling out racism and gaslighting, the latter being the title of one of his songs. I've said this during many interviews, but he had no reason to and would not receive any secondary gain from talking to me, aside from doing so out of the goodness of his heart. For example, Guy already has millions of followers across all his social media platforms and is likely bombarded with many interview requests. I was so impressed by his response to my question in Clubhouse about ways that mental health is addressed, or not, among the Asian American community and on the show, "Bling Empire." I later followed up with a direct message to invite him on the show, and he agreed! I cannot gush enough about Guy Tang. He is a sweetheart who loves and cares about others and will also speak with honesty and openness. So, if you value someone's thoughts and perspective, tell them, and ask them to connect because you never know where it will lead you. My interview with Melody You, creator of the digital art series, "Album Receipts," reinforced this notion when she shared that her viral sensations were inspired by a person who created a receipt of an album cover. She contacted him and he was supportive of her putting her own spin on it.

I've recently learned that celebrity is subjective, and all guests who have come on the show are amazing people and leaders. We look for a guest who is willing to be vulnerable while sharing their journey and

Cancel the Filter

providing ways to cope with stressors and challenges. We also gauge if a proposed guest has listened to the show on our guest request form and whether they have a genuine interest in sharing a message that is consistent with our, "Why." Pro tip: A person likely has not engaged with the content if they respond, with "All of them," or "Have not listened to one yet, but like what you are doing" to the question, "What is your favorite episode?" For example, I encouraged myself to take the same risk that Dr. Varghese communicated during the master class—move out of your comfort zone because it leads to more growth, despite the hurdles. This book is a tangible way that I am doing so.

After a little over five months, we reached the milestone of 1,000 downloads after one of our closest friends listened to the William Hung episode. While for some, this may seem small, it was huge for a podcast that started out of obscurity. This meant more people than my mom were listening to the show! Even though I try not to look at the metrics, they did motivate me to work harder. At this point, I was exhausted and feeling burnt out, as indicated by my feeling sluggish, not wanting to work as much in my private practice, and hiding in my glam room while my family watched television. I am an introvert-extrovert and often need time to recharge, especially since I feel like I must be on all the time. I am beyond grateful that my family always accommodates me and treats me like a queen. Early on in life, my husband taught our children "not to bother Mommy" before she wakes up. How amazing is that?

The podcast's purpose was further magnified after it was reported that Asian American hate crimes skyrocketed 350% in early 2021, and the brutal incidents were plastered all over social media. The murder of Vicha Ratanapakdee, an 84-year-old, Thai immigrant who was pushed to his death, sparked a nationwide movement. Many of us took to our platforms to highlight the incidents and call for change and action, particularly since we feared for the safety of community members, our elders being the most at risk of being attacked. This was a collective way to demonstrate that we would not be silent and are just as American as anyone else. Our children deserve to grow up in a welcoming and safe environment.

Asian American celebrities, including Margaret Cho, also began utilizing their social media platforms to speak out. #StopAAPIHate,

#StopAsianHate, and #Hateisavirus became the hashtags that were widely utilized to raise awareness. Serendipitously, a notification on Clubhouse popped up from PK Comedy with the room name something to the effect of, "Sex Jokes with Margaret Cho." PK and I had recently connected because our children had made innocent drawings of Legos and a Blackpink lightstick, but they looked like phallic symbols. I entered the room and was luckily one of the first brought on stage. I mentioned the story and told everyone that I was hiding in my glam room so my kids could not hear this conversation, and while I loved a good dick joke, I also wanted to ask Margaret about mental health. I "shot my shot," and invited her on the show. She agreed, and I just hoped that would still be the case when I slid into her DMs, and to my surprise, she responded immediately to schedule the interview. Never in my wildest dreams would I have imagined interviewing an icon who demonstrated that an Asian American-led television show, "All-American Girl" was possible. This was a show that my dad and I watched before I went to bed, and aside from my parents being proud of me interviewing her, I was grateful that she was bringing more awareness to the issue at hand and communicating a message of hope.

Overall, the most important motivator for continuing the podcast was how important the show was to Oz. One day, after school, she was brimming with excitement, "I told Ms. Teacher about your podcast. She listened to it and said she liked it!" The pride on her face was indescribable, and she translated that pride into her Women's History Month presentation. Students were asked to include slides, detailing a woman they admired. She surprised me by writing about me and the podcast, and how it was so cool that I interviewed people. I will bring this back up when she is a teenager that she thought I was cool. Her teacher was not the only one whom she encouraged to listen to the show. When school transitioned back to a hybrid model and my husband brought the kids to work for the virtual portion, Oz would talk to my husband's co-worker about the show and repeatedly ask him if he listened to it, which he eventually did. We literally have our own in-house PR! There was also one day when I was so burnt out that I had a throw-up-your-hands moment. I said aloud, "I want to quit the podcast." Oz turned towards me, shocked, with eyes wide open, and said, "You want to *quit* the podcast? Why, Mommy?"

I guess I'm not.

Lessons Learned:

Sponsorship

Many podcasters examine their options to monetize their podcast or use it as marketing funnels for other goods and services. In fact, in Asian American culture, the common question when starting an endeavor is, "How are you going to monetize?" I did not start the podcast to make money and I did not need to up-sell any products or services. However, the mindset was still to hustle, and because we were so new, we did not have the downloads to make more than a few cents on the hosting platform we used. One day, my impulsivity took over and I moved our podcast to another platform because you could play ads with any download numbers. I learned a lesson after it led to an error in posting on one of the major distribution channels. Then when I moved it back to our original platform, the reviews disappeared! I was frantic and emailed various services to help. Eventually, it was resolved but I learned a lesson to slow down. It was also a clear reminder that I was not doing this for money, but for individuals' stories to be told, and to have the stories resonate with listeners.

Instead of relying on general monetization practices, I began to think outside the box. Since the pandemic led many to deliver and seek treatment via telehealth, many recruiters were reaching out to me to join their organizations. While I was very flattered, I have dedicated myself to an exclusive contract with a company because they have continually shown to value my time and skill via reimbursement rates and ease of submitting claims. But I still wanted to work with various companies that were trying to make changes in the mental health field so I politely declined the recruiter's initial offer and asked if they would like to sponsor an episode or more. This led to our first monetary sponsorship!

I have also been extremely grateful to guests who also provide us with sponsored merchandise that we utilize for raffles and building mutual brand awareness. Money is nice, but it is not everything. It is really about building relationships. One of the mantras that I live by is, "The most valuable currency is relationships."

There have been so many amazing partners! One of the most rewarding products came from Angel Halo Chang, the author of the children's book, *You Are Invited!* She generously gave a signed copy to Oz's class and her teacher read it aloud. We also had a singer/musician perform her interpretation of the story on the podcast. The book celebrates diversity and will now be a part of the school's library for years to come. We have given away Passion Planners, artwork, and dog treats. What I love to see and hear are stories of ethnic minority authors, artists, entrepreneurs, and doctors who are paving the way for our children to do meaningful things with their lives.

Social Comparison is a Bitch

Yes, I said it! After all, this book is about addressing social media's false lens of our lives. Many people will make posts about not comparing yourself to others and "just keep doing what you are doing." This has been extremely difficult for me because, like many of you, I have social media and fortunately, friends. In fact, in many Asian American families, parents and elders will compare children based on the children's perceived abilities and grades. As they grow up, other comparison points are degrees, jobs, income, family life, material possessions, etc. Dr. Jenny Wang, founder of Asians for Mental Health, defined the concept of the zero-sum game, or the notion that only one person/family can succeed or win. She noted that while it was adaptive for earlier generations of Asian immigrants to maintain their businesses and purchase homes, this mindset can now lead to tearing down others because you feel you need to win. Guy Tang discussed this in his interview, and I have observed it on social media. For example, William Hung sang his heart out on American Idol and had no regrets. However, even years later, another

Cancel the Filter

famous Asian American celebrity criticized him for "setting Asian Americans back." William Hung's intention was not to become a caricature of the AAPI community. He was getting out of his comfort zone by trying something new, and I am proud of him.

To be fair, social comparison is not a solely Asian American phenomenon. We see it everywhere—magazines, television, streaming platforms, and news outlets, projecting beauty and behavioral standards. There is also a lot to be said of individuals and groups of people not represented in the media. I can count on one hand, the number of lead Asian American actresses I saw on television throughout my childhood and adolescence. I realize now why Trini, or the Yellow Power Ranger, was so important to me. Combine these social factors with an inherent motivation to achieve in activities that I care about, and you will have a lifelong struggle with perfectionism.

Here is the thing about perfectionism. Rationally, we know that no one is perfect. However, we use external markers as metrics of success. In my youth, I thought having a degree, six-figure job, a house, and luxury brand items equated to success. This seems extremely materialistic, but I am compassionate towards my younger self because to her, growing up in a single-income family, these markers seemed to be something to strive for. Over the years, with support from my family, friends, colleagues, and therapist, I have become a lot more flexible about my definition of success than I was in my youth. Even with all the self-reflection and support, perfectionism is a feeling or thinking trap that is pervasive and intense.

A trigger occurred when I first started podcasting in 2020, or the Year of Suck due to the pandemic. A friend was building a community and had an amazing idea of having an awards ceremony for Asian American podcasters. I threw our name in the hat for a few categories, hoping we would get nominated in at least one of them. My husband and I filmed the nomination video in our bathroom about the podcast and our team. Of course, our editor did his magic, and it did not look like a hot mess like the raw footage. The nominees were revealed, and we received a nomination for the "Best Wellness Podcast" category. I did not have high expectations when I was submitting the nomination form, but when I saw our podcast on the ballot, my competitiveness kicked in. Members of the group could now vote and there would be a deadline to join the group. I started doing work, contacting previous guests, friends, and family to see if they could join and vote. I was extremely grateful as I saw my friends and family's names on the new members lists, but it also fueled my drive to win.

The night of the awards came, and our category was announced later in the program. I put on my eyelashes and a dress, which was very uncharacteristic of pandemic fashion. When our category was announced, I was sitting in anticipation. Then when I heard our show won silver, I began to bawl. Fortunately, only the host of the show who won gold was invited onto the virtual stage because I was a hot mess! A lot of thoughts flooded into my head, none of which had anything to do with the other shows because I knew they were amazing. More so, I questioned why didn't all our hard work pay off? Why did I involve my friends and family only to come up short? I was a psychologist in a wellness category, why couldn't we have won? Do you see a theme in the self-directed questions? Meanwhile, others were congratulating us on winning silver, but that night, it was hard to quiet the self-deprecation. As my husband later pointed out, "You hate losing." His observation comes with over twenty years of data so yes, I would say that is fairly accurate.

A few days later, a friend and previous guest who I had contacted to support us for the vote, apologized for seeing the message past the deadline to vote. She congratulated me on the award, and laughed at my lackluster response, stating, "Is it because you didn't win gold? Ha Ha." I started smiling from ear to ear because I could always rely on her for real talk. Her question re-centered me, and while being publicly acknowledged is an honor within itself, basing my worth on an external award or achievement does not actually bring me joy. As the Rock says, "It's nice to be important, but more important to be nice."

While it feels very vulnerable and embarrassing to share the awards incident, it is also authentic. It reminds me and others that we are human, and it is a human experience to manage expectations of self and others. A book that has helped me manage my expectations is Leo Tolstoy's *The Death of Ivan Illyich*. A judge, Ivan, is on his deathbed when he reflects on his life of propriety, trying to live his according to perceived societal standards, and striving to assume a level of authority over others. His work and desire to advance his career consumed his life. One day, he was hanging curtains, a perceived symbol of status because everyone who was successful around him had some variation of these curtains. He fell while hanging these prized curtains, hitting his head on the doorknob, which led to the deterioration of his health and ultimate death. My takeaway from the story is to not hang your curtains. In all seriousness, living your life strictly by perceived societal, capitalist standards will not coincide with joy or contentment, and oftentimes you will miss out on being present with your loved ones. This is not to say, do not have any external goals in your life. But rather examine the intentions behind your goals and where you direct your time to ensure you are living consistently with your values. To me, success means being able to have loving, strong relationships with family, friends, and myself, and providing for our needs while engaging in self-care. I strive for the freedom and privilege to give our kids opportunities that I didn't have, and to be able to do what I want to do when I want to do it, within reason. Don't get it twisted, you need money for things of that nature, but it does not mean equating my worth to external achievements. This is a notion that I have to continue to unlearn. A Disney+ documentary, *Suga: Road to D-Day,* reinforces the notion that material possessions do not equate to happiness. Loosely translated, BTS' Suga stated, "We think about making it big, making money, buying watches and nice cars and everything. But none of those things are what makes your life fun. You might say, 'Hey you made it big, that's why you can say that.' Yes, that's why I can tell you that they're not the fun part. But when I meet up with people and make music, that's fun."

Golden Crane Awards, Asian American Podcast Association

It was the second year that I had submitted a nomination at the Golden Crane Awards. In 2020, we were fortunate to be accepted as an official nominee. In 2021, we also became an official nominee for "Best Mental Health Podcast." I didn't have high expectations, considering we had yet to win a first-place award. After going back and forth with Ya Ya about the dress to wear to the virtual ceremony, the kids and I sat patiently and waited for our category. This time felt different. When they were about to announce the winner, I thought, "This category was made for us."

"The Golden Crane for the Best Mental Health Podcast goes to... The Color of Success!"

The kids whooped and pretended to accept the trophy as the gorgeous crystal trophy with gold lettering would be mailed to the winners. I can't dictate my speech word for word, but it went something like this, "Thank you so much! This award belongs to Victor, Ronald, Elizabeth, Peter, Oz, and Ya Ya."

I could tell the co-host was getting impatient, but I knew my speech would get better.

"This award belongs to all of you and all the hard work you do to put out stories. As BTS says, 'If our existence can combat xenophobia...' So, let's keep creating great content and give voice to our stories."

In the chat, folks were super encouraging, saying that my kids were able to see their mother rock and that I delivered a good speech.

After submitting the writing for the engraving and receiving the award, I proudly took pictures with it and of it. The recognition and love we received, and the ability to connect with other award winners, nominees, and community members have been amazing!

That same night, my dad asked to talk to me on the phone privately. *Cryptic much?* The conversation started very positively, telling me that they placed an offer on a huge house an hour away from my brother and his work. I quickly clicked on the link and the status was pending. I was so happy for them because they never imagined owning a home.

Apparently, my dad had been in the hospital since the day before we spoke and only told me now because my brother had urged him to. His legs and feet were swollen, his lung had a blood clot, and he was told that he had a weak heart. He had to undergo an angiogram, and he detailed the risks. Then he engaged in a conversation that no loving child wants to talk about—his assets in case he didn't make it through the procedure. I quickly told him to leave it all to my brother, but he told me the percentage splits. I began bawling because it seemed so surreal, like a nightmare. He told me to help my brother with finances.

Cancel the Filter

"We are in such a good place in our relationship."

"I know," he said soothingly.

My dad communicated his dreams for us. For me, an internationally successful podcast and to be able to meet and interview BTS. I joked, "I want to be friends with them." For my husband, to manage multiple properties. For my brother, to run his own franchise in the food industry and enjoy their home. For his granddaughters, he observed that they were only "scratching the surface of their greatness."

"I don't want to miss a thing," he said.

Initially, we thought he needed a stent, but further tests revealed he needed a valve replacement. Following the surgery, he would be unable to drive for six weeks. We eventually told the girls so they wouldn't jump on him. He kept reassuring us that everything was going to be fine and checked on me after he told me. Of course, he comforted me when he deserved the comfort and worry. Our family commonly uses humor to cope, or else we would cry all the time. We kept half-joking as to who would help him shower.

My father stayed with us for six weeks and made a full recovery. He was the perfect patient, ambulating very quickly, and cooking his own healthy meals. In fact, we had to tell him to slow down. He was walking two dogs in no time and miles around the neighborhood. His determination and the support of the family led him to return to his new home and eventually return to work.

Be My Guest (cue Lumière from *Beauty and the Beast*)

One of the most special things about podcasting is being invited as a guest on other folks' podcasts, a panelist or speaker, and making new friends and connections. I have been able to share my own story and provide my professional and personal opinions, which has made me feel connected to the hosts even though I have yet to meet many of them in person. For those who are looking to grow their audience, collaborating with friends on their platforms is a fun and effective way to do so. Being a part of a community of content creators has been uplifting because content creation can be a lonely journey if you let it be. I have learned to hone my skills as a host by being in the opposite seat and responding to different styles of interviewing. I've found that some hosts are free-flowing and some are semi-structured.

On "Dear Asian Americans," my friend, Tiffany Hwang was the guest host for the month and invited four Asian American women onto the show that inspired her. I was honored to be one of them. The founder, Jerry Won, asks guests to author a letter, beginning, "Dear Asian Americans..." I wrote my letter in chicken scratch while journaling at 12:00 or 1:00 a.m. I wanted to get all my thoughts down and type it concisely. It was very therapeutic for me to write a letter in the context of the Anti-Asian sentiment that was rampant at the time because I continued to feel mixed emotions, one of which was helplessness. I have included my letter as a source of hope.

Dear Asian Americans,

It is okay to seek help from a psychologist/mental health provider. I mean, psychologists are doctors, too! In all seriousness, it is a strength to seek help and not a weakness. Therapy is not some mystical event and does not mean you are crazy. It gives you a confidential, safe space to talk about things that may be bothering you. You also do not have to necessarily exhibit moderate to severe issues but may need assistance managing daily stressors and exploring self-development.

Right now, many of us are going through pain on a community level, and I am encouraging you to speak your truth, reach out to those you love, and connect with community members across various ethnicities because now is an important time in history. We are at a fork in the road to choose solidarity and understanding over divisiveness. Be curious about what other people's struggles/journeys are. Just as many of us hope that we are not viewed as sole representatives of our ethnic/racial groups for bad behavior, we need to practice this notion when viewing events. It is not a time to put our heads down and fly under the radar, but to speak up for our rights to safety, justice, and equality.

Do not give up because there are people who will lift you up [like Tiffany and myself]. If we want to create a better place for our children and loved ones, now is the time to get involved in advocacy, increasing

Cancel the Filter

diversity and representation, elevating our voices in all sectors of society, encouraging our teachers to include Asian American history and books by Asian American authors in the curriculum, being active in the community and social justice organizations, and moderating social media groups, etc. We have the power and will to create positive change.
 With gratitude,
 Stephanie

Podfest

Podfest is one of the largest, if not the largest podcast convention in the country. Due to the pandemic, it was virtual, and I submitted a proposal to speak at the Asian American Podcasters (AAP) Association session at the event. It was accepted, but I had to be on a call during a family trip to Tahoe. I was torn because I had sent an email letting the committee know that I was away, and I was looking forward to touching base with them on another day. However, I did not hear from the organizers, so I was urging myself to stay present while building a snowman in front of the condo and debating whether or not to hop onto the call, which I eventually did in the car. Fortunately, it was a quick call and I stayed on afterward to discuss more logistics. I would likely be paired with another presenter, which was exciting because it is great to have a solid collaborator. It so happened to be another fellow nominee in the best wellness award category.

My partner and I connected instantly, and now I call her a soul sister! She was so real, and it was refreshing because she supported me throughout the process. I sent my draft slides for the presentation, and she provided me with honest feedback. We felt immense pressure to turn around the content in a short amount of time and clearly present the information. As we were preparing, I recalled what BM from the K-pop group, Kard said, "If you are going to work in entertainment, be flexible. Things change all the time. Timetables can be tight." While I do not consider myself in entertainment in any sense, I believe flexibility is key in most sectors where you are working with people.

Have you observed my Type A tendencies? I have learned that this does not mean I am doomed to be inflexible, but rather, I must put in extra effort and self-awareness to go against my nature in certain situations to behave in a manner consistent with my goals and values. Therefore, I tend to place myself in situations that are conducive to pushing back on these tendencies when needed. Some examples of this include, I chose to attend a college that offered a rigorous curriculum but had an overall, laid-back culture. While I went to a magnet high school, there was also the freedom to create your own schedule by choosing which classes you took at what periods and with which teachers. You did not always understand who you were or what you preferred, but it was modeled after the college system and made the transition from high school to college relatively smooth.

As I've progressed throughout my life, I have realized that like many, I am a walking paradox. I may take comfort in some sense of structure, but I also value flexibility in my schedule. For example, setting deadlines is important, but it does not matter how you get your work done, which is consistent with Netflix's company culture of freedom and responsibility.

On the day of the conference, I had slight jitters, but before any presentation, I tend to have the jitters and they dissipate when I get into my flow. I knew the material because I had done my usual routine of practicing in front of my oldest dog, as well as once while I was on the exercise bike, and once with my soul sister. The last part of the confidence package is to work on the visuals. I spent my morning using my mermaid crimper on my hair, putting on my "It's Okay not to be Okay," K-drama-inspired dress, and earth-toned makeup. I'm biased, but we slayed it with our presentation, "Got Podcast Burnout? Maintaining Motivation to Your First 1,000 Downloads." The best part about Podfest was making new friends, contributing to Asian American representation in podcasting and media, learning from presenters, and joining a larger community of supportive people.

Cancel the Filter

It's Okay Not to be Okay Panel

A post about a new audio app led to a journalist reaching out to me, inviting me on a panel of DJs, musicians, a comedian, and a journalist about mental health. The panel was to raise money for When the Music Stops, an organization that seeks to help others cope with mental health issues, particularly those in the music industry. I never thought I would be on such an exciting panel. I was taught to give presentations at academic conferences and publish articles in peer-reviewed journals, not necessarily to prepare for a panel with entertainers. I immediately nicknamed comedian Donnell Rawlings, my Walking Antidepressant because he is hilarious and spoke with such honesty about the stigma of help-seeking in the Black and African American community. Professor Bun B provided so many gems and everything he said was so impactful and thoughtful. He received extra brownie points from me because when we were asked to introduce ourselves, he said, "I'll let the doctor go first." I acknowledged how powerful it was that he invited and encouraged an Asian American woman to speak first. That act is a powerful example of how to encourage equity and ensure everyone's voices are heard.

Other powerful discussions included one DJ telling the audience that he was not on speaking terms with his mother because she was a QAnon member even though she was an immigrant. Another DJ poignantly discussed racial tensions throughout the country and the personal impact it has had on him. I added my perspective of the frequent and severe Asian hate crimes being committed and the Anti-Asian sentiment that is pervasive in society even today.

Continued Education

During the pandemic, I read more books than I had in many years. Since childhood, I loved to read, losing myself in Nancy Drew mysteries and any books my fifth-grade teacher assigned. While I was scared shitless reading books by Mary Higgins Clark, they were so engrossing. As I went through high school, college, and graduate school, reading became a chore, as I pored over research papers and textbooks. When I was accepted into graduate school, and I no longer needed to perform to reach the next step, I briefly enjoyed reading again because it was no longer a requirement.

During the pandemic, I read Jim Kwik's *Limitless*, which discusses "learning about learning;" Kevin Kwan's *Sex and Vanity*, Ta-Nehisi Coates' *Between the World and Me*, a deep and thoughtful long-form letter to his son, examining the construct of race and the implications of conceptualizations of race; Kamala Harris's *The Truths We Hold*, Cathy Park Hong's *Minor Feelings*, and Marc Randolph's *That Will Never Work*, detailing the founding of Netflix. These books provided me with a different perspective on life, relationships, race, and business. Marc's book led me to reflect on our family's keys to success, as he detailed his own. On a side note, Marc is a compassionate and thoughtful man, not only evidenced by the content of his book. I learned this firsthand after I DM'd him on Instagram to tell him how much I liked his book and to be cautious about calling Asian food weird. To my surprise, he wrote back, "Thanks, Stephanie. Glad you liked the book. And sorry about the language—I'm still working on recognizing all the places where bias exists. I'm just working on trying each day to keep getting better. Thanks for pointing it out."

I now understand why so many people want to work for and with him. I was even more motivated to understand what messages I had internalized and shared with my family. I also continue to work on combating my drive to achieve—achieving is subjective—and the biases that I hold based on my levels of privilege.

Keys to Success:

- Build relationships and connect with others who are genuine, supportive, kind, intelligent, and willing to mutually assist each other.

Cancel the Filter

- Prioritize your family and loved ones and show them you care in a variety of ways (texts, cards, gifts, hugs within appropriate boundaries, saying "I love you," spending quality time together, helping them with something).
- Treat people with respect regardless of their ethnicity, religion, gender, sexual orientation, relationship status, mobility, etc.
- Prioritize your mental and physical health, which includes taking breaks, vacations, exercising, eating as healthy as you can, taking vitamins and/or medications (if needed), engaging in hobbies, going to medical and mental health appointments, and identifying strategies that can help get you through tough times.
- Have a hobby that has nothing to do with making money or that feels like work.
- Dedicate your time to projects, jobs, and activities that give you meaning.
- Work hard with boundaries and self-care.
- Do not undervalue what you can bring to your team and organization, and make sure to show up for yourself.
- Advocacy and assertiveness are key (e.g., in negotiating salaries and benefits, taking on projects with increased visibility).
- Engage in self-reflection.
- Set goals that are consistent with your values, and monitor your progress and what you can do to continue moving towards your values.
- Ask questions if you do not know something and if elaboration would be helpful to you.
- Do not ask someone to do something that you wouldn't do yourself or wouldn't be willing to learn.
- Do not be afraid to admit a mistake.
- Dream big and put in the hard work to realize your dreams (this also takes a bit of luck).
- Treat yourself.

- Manage your money to maximize your income and maintain a budget to help with goal setting.

In the middle of 2021, I was contacted by Ira Sukrungruang's team. Ira is the author of various books, and they specifically wanted me to discuss his soon-to-be-released book, *This Jade World*. I was thrilled that I received a copy upon my request, delving into the world of a Thai American man pre-and post-divorce. I practiced a speed-reading technique that I learned from Jim Kwik's book and didn't have to try hard at all to be engaged in the book because it was fantastic. While Ira noted that he cringes and strongly dislikes talking about the subject of sex, he opens the book with a sexual interaction. During the interview, the first question I asked him was, "Ira, you are immediately vulnerable in the opening of the book, starting with your least favorite topic—sex. What inspired you to be so vulnerable throughout the entire book?"

He noted, "I tell my students when they write memoirs—confront that which makes you most uncomfortable. Most people avoid discomfort." He initially avoided it.

We both agreed that if he did not confront topics of sex, weight consciousness, and his relationships, the book and his narrative would not have the same level of depth. I was happy to see multiple facets of his life, culture, and identity addressed. He also encourages his students to focus on the process of writing and not on the physical product of a published piece. This helped kick-start me to continue writing this book.

Ira also discussed synchronicity, which I felt that day during the interview. Post-divorce and during the pandemic, BTS facilitated joy again, which led to discussing our collection of BTS dolls, and who our biases are. He also wrote the book where his mother and deceased aunt resided in Chiang Mai, a place where my husband and I bonded significantly, and also where I got my second tattoo, paying homage to my children. The universe is connected.

*　*　*

Cancel the Filter

Joseph J. Lam is an entrepreneur who co-created the game, Parents Are Human, which is a bilingual connection card game designed to help immigrant families have deeper conversations and forge stronger ties. He sought to heal a broken and distant relationship with his parents, as there was an emotional wall between them. Through the creation and implementation of the game, he built intimacy with his parents and learned that due to his mother living through the Chinese Famine, she expresses her love through the food she prepares for the family. Before playing the game, he often became frustrated when she gave him three portions worth of food, despite his objection. He now has a better understanding of why food is so important to share with loved ones.

Joseph reached out to me to send me a deck, writing, "Absolutely free and I expect nothing in return." My love for free things prompted me to say, "Yes," immediately. The game includes seventy prompts with two levels of difficulty to inspire connection, compassion, and vulnerability. Each card includes a question or action in English on the front and either Chinese, Vietnamese, Spanish, Korean, Tagalog, and several more languages on the back to help bridge language, cultural, or generational gaps.

I only knew about the game through what was detailed on the website and in our shared Asian American social media group. What transpired when we played the game was amazing. I played with my family, and I learned new things about my husband that I never knew in the past twenty years. I shared my favorite memory of my mother with her, which was when she took my brother and me to "meet" the Power Rangers at Toys R Us. We didn't have a lot of money, but my mother always wanted us to have the latest toys and experiences, so we lined up to meet our heroes. When it was my family's turn to meet the Power Rangers, who were lined up in front of the diaper section, we got an autographed black-and-white photo.

The Power Rangers were the most diverse actors that we had at the time, including an Asian woman who played Trini, the Yellow Ranger. The Power Rangers meant that my friends could dress up as characters that looked like them. I could pretend to be the Yellow Ranger. My mixed-raced best friend, who resembled Kimberly, could play the role of the Pink Ranger. I remember how I couldn't wait until the next school day to tell my friends all about my experience.

As I enthusiastically told my friends about my exciting meet-and-greet, one of my friends said, "You didn't meet the Power Rangers."

"Yes, I did," I insisted.

"No, you didn't. Did they take off their helmets?" she countered.

I paused. "No."

"Then you didn't meet them," she said matter-of-factly. "I met them," she said as she handed me a picture of the actors with their helmets off.

I wasn't embarrassed, but more so confused. I later went home and asked my mom, "Did you know that they weren't the real Power Rangers?"

She played it off really well, "No, I didn't know."

During dinner, my brother and I heard on the news that the Power Rangers were at the hotel where my friend went to meet them.

During the Parents Are Human game, I asked my mom, "Did you know they were fake?"

"Hell, yeah, I knew," she laughed.

When it was my mother's turn to share her memory, she began crying, noting, "I can't think of a positive memory of my mother," which was like both her brothers. It provides context as to why she wanted us to have everything she didn't have growing up.

* * *

I later played with my dad who named me the most influential person in his life.

"Me?" I said in utter disbelief.

He explained that he was proud of how I turned out, despite all that I've been through, and that I'm very forgiving. I hugged him with tears in my eyes.

It wasn't all tears, and when I asked what the scariest moment was in his life, Oz blurted out, "When you got married to Grandma?"

We all started laughing!

I later offered to highlight Joseph as a sponsor of an episode and invited him on the show as a guest. I joked, "I wanted to play the game first before inviting you because what if it sucked?" In all seriousness, it is an amazing game and tool, and I often recommend it to those who are looking to strengthen or improve family dynamics.

Meeting IRL (in real life): Learning to Socialize Again

As more people were vaccinated against COVID-19, it opened up the possibility to meet people IRL that I met virtually through podcasting. Meeting people IRL was like going on a first date in terms of awkwardness. For me, it was an adjustment to socialize in person without intuitively knowing what to say by typing it. From a psychological perspective, I imagine socializing without a screen has been an adjustment for many people. My husband never forgot how to socialize IRL, so he always helps ease any tension there is when meeting new people.

When the Music Stops Summit

The "It's Okay Not to be Okay Panel" opened a door for me. The panel sought to fundraise for the organization When the Music Stops (WTMS), which seeks to promote suicide prevention and mental health. It was founded by Joshua Donaldson, a promoter for his friend and colleague, Avicii, who died by suicide. Joshua engaged in a year of inpatient mental health treatment to cope with loss and mental health issues. He invited me to speak at the second annual summit of When the Music Stops, merging music, healing, and mental health.

* * *

After I received the invitation, I asked my husband to accompany me because he eases my stranger anxiety, and I would feel safer going to the city with him, given the rise in Asian hate crimes. Words cannot express how grateful I am for his attendance because he is my comfort person, safe attachment, and has absolutely no jealousy or resentment about being there for me. In fact, he introduced himself as, "The husband." The funny thing is, when we got our participation badges, he was stoked that he got his very own "staff" badge, especially since that meant access to all the free snacks and drinks. We may have to battle it out as to who is the cheapest in the family, but he may take the title of "Ultimate Cheapskate" in our immediate family. I often send him clips of the show, *Ultimate Cheapskate* as a joke.

I didn't know what to expect because the planning for this event was a bit haphazard. But one of the lessons I learned is that in the music/entertainment industry, a show will happen in a big way. It was a gorgeous event with red leather armchairs on the stage for the panelists, a gray seat for the moderator, a DJ booth on the right-hand side of the stage, mic/sound engineers backstage, Waiting and Green rooms, interviewers, camera persons, and a flurry of invited speakers and guests. After the many DMs we exchanged, I hugged Josh for the first time IRL. He was about to open the show in half an hour, and there was some anticipatory anxiety. However, once he got on stage, it was like a flip was switched and he was hyped.

Josh opened the show with a warm, excited welcome, pacing the stage slowly, and engaging the audience. He asked, "Why are you here? What do you hope to get out of the summit?"

My husband later showed me his response in his WTMS notebook —"I'm an Uber driver." We had a good laugh.

On a more serious note, one audience member raised her hand and began to choke up, stating that she lost a close friend to suicide within the past week. Josh empathically and supportively stated, "Your friend is with us today."

Backstage, it felt awkward to introduce myself to a whole bunch of people who would likely not remember my name, but I pushed myself out of my comfort zone, attempting to connect with others. I am so glad that I did! My other panelists tasked with addressing mental health in communities of color, as well as others I met, were inspiring, positive, and kind people. Theo Ellington, the director of the Salvation Army, and who previously ran for political office, was a Bay Area native and a father. We actually discovered that the four of us panelists were Bay Area natives. It was synchronicity that Josh had grouped us together. I immediately connected with Karl Watson who is a Black, pro skater sponsored by Adidas and the author of the children's book, *My First Skateboard*. Yes, I am name-dropping because my fellow panelists deserve to be recognized! Malik Adunni was also releasing his book, inspired by his family's history, *Malik's Magic African Alphabet Hat*, and he was wearing a shirt with "Amplify" across the chest, conveying multiple meanings. Malik spoke of culture, family, and diversity, all while ensuring that the panelists were where they were supposed to be and had a working mic.

Backstage as the DJ paid homage to the anniversary of Biz Markie's passing, each panelist was handed a mic. Dr. Alfiee Breland-Noble, the moderator for the panel, and I swayed as we joined in with the audience, "You. You got what I neeeed. You say he's just a friend. You say he just a friend. Oh, baby, you!"

Josh debriefed us on the seating arrangement, and as the panel was introduced, I walked out, waved, and smiled for the cameras as my other co-panelists and Dr. Alfiee joined me on stage. Dr. Alfiee then asked us to re-introduce ourselves.

"I'm Dr. Stephanie *J*. Wong, and I emphasize the J. because there are a million Stephanie Wongs. I get their emails and medical notes."

While it got a good laugh from the audience, Josh now introduces me this way, partly because he was apologetic for leaving it out of the promo packages.

As the introductions rounded out, Dr. Alfiee asked, "What does mental health mean to you?"

"Harmony, family, growth, and friendship. Shout-out to my husband. We recently celebrated twenty-one years," I said, as the audience applauded.

Co-panelists elaborated on issues of race, race relations, and being unapologetic for being a minority in a specific industry.

Dr. Alfiee turned her gaze to me. "Are there considerations in Asian American/Asian American Pacific Islander communities regarding mental health (not to over-generalize)?"

"There has been an increase in hate crimes and stigma in discussing mental health issues. We have a right to be respected, seen, and heard. I'm unapologetically assertive (reframed from annoying). I work with individuals in leadership who are White and there may be an expectation that I will be timid," I answered.

Dr. Alfiee's closing question was, "What do you do to take care of your mental health?"

"I karaoke every day. I do K-pop and American songs. I am a member of the BTS ARMY even before they made English songs. I also detach by watching trashy TV to lessen the weight of carrying others' issues and pondering the complexities of human behavior. Sometimes, I don't want to think. It's okay to detach," I said.

Karl mentioned that he liked being in nature. Robin, a music/entertainment industry veteran, stated that she enjoys being with her family, despite the chaos. Theo discussed the disappointment of losing a 2018 local election and how he built up a wall of isolation. He began to feel motivated to engage in activism again with the rising racial tensions and discrimination (e.g., the murder of George Floyd) while being mindful that he has a two-year-old son so he cannot protest in front of trains right now. Dr. Alfiee closed the panel by asking everyone to sing, "Happy Birthday" to her daughter who accompanied her to the summit, which demonstrated that her family was of the utmost importance to having a fulfilling life.

Backstage, I had been holding in my pee even before the panel but continued to do so because Josh instructed us to do our individual interviews. The interview room was reminiscent of the "Real World" confessional interviews. The interviewer and cameraman kindly guided me through the interview, and he gave me positive feedback, reasoning that I have my own podcast so I would be comfortable doing an interview. I found that I had become less nervous on camera due to the shift during the pandemic to daily virtual calls, enabling me to monitor my facial expressions. Apparently, podcasting has been an investment in my personal and professional development.

The panel with veteran music industry professionals was amazing, and I was particularly impressed by the producer of "Dead & Gone" with Justin Timberlake. He spoke of the start and progression of his career, noting that he was Egyptian, and "If we could build pyramids,

Cancel the Filter

we could do anything." He mentioned that his family is comprised of lawyers, doctors, and his brother is an aeronautical engineer. When he told them he was not going to college and going to make beats, they thought he was weird.

"To this day, many of my family still think I'm a DJ. My brother asked me if I could DJ his wedding and I told him, 'No. I'm the Best Man and I'm not a DJ.'"

Josh asked, "What was the best piece of advice you would like to give your younger self?"

"Validate yourself, dumbass," Rob replied.

I later told Rob that we should ask Josh to make bumper stickers of the quote.

Another stand-out panelist to me was Jeremiah who worked with 50 Cent for over a decade, starting as an intern and working his way up the ladder with the guidance of a mentor. Hilariously, Jeremiah wore shorts that spelled, "HEAL" on the leg. He said that he lost the "L," which my husband later found. He also lost the "A," but he found that himself. He slowly and deliberately spoke of the loss of his mentor to suicide and another to sickle cell. He found hope and healing by working with children who were diagnosed with autism, "wiping their a*s and doing things that I wasn't prepared to do." He wanted to help others because his mentor's advocacy on his behalf had helped him tremendously.

Musical performances throughout the show were nothing short of amazing. My co-panelist, Nina Grae moved the crowd with her singing performance. She exuded Alicia Keys vibes when she spoke to the audience between songs. She integrated healing, hope, and love into her performances and songs. While I listened to Jane the Messenger as she sang, "Shut the F*ck Up" faster and faster, I thought, *I need this chorus so I can press it when I'm annoyed with someone.* She laughed when I told her later and disclosed that she was diagnosed with autism and has difficulty picking up social cues. As a result, she dances in her own world on stage.

I assured Jane, "At least you don't get nervous."

Jim Kwik's tip for networking is to identify one to two people who you want to make it a point to meet by the end of a conference. For me, it was Nikki Blades as I watched her and Timothy Chantarangsu on the "No Chaser Podcast." It was enlightening to hear her talk about the insecurity of putting her work out there as opposed to a picture in a bikini because she is comfortable with negative criticism about her body. She also advised the audience to post content that they would be comfortable with their employer seeing, which is a great rule of thumb.

As Dr. Alfiee said, "You use social media. Don't let social media use you."

Ben Baller, a luxury jeweler to celebrities and a father of three who mean the world to him, was also on the panel. He pleasantly surprised me with his bluntness and hilarity, reminding me of my husband. Therefore, I was hoping to connect with both Nikki and Ben.

After the panel, the lounge was empty, so I went upstairs to pee. They were all in the dressing room! I silently cursed myself because I gave my phone to my husband to hold. I invisibly walked through the circle to use the restroom, and I peed hurriedly, worried that I would waste an opportunity. After washing up, I first hugged Dr. Radisha, the moderator, particularly since we connected on social media before the panel. I then turned to Nikki and managed to ask her how her sister was recovering from a heart condition she developed post-partum. She said that streaming made her sister feel less lonely.

Another person offered that she would like to post bikini pictures herself, but she did not want to open herself up to others' expectations of her body.

"I want to post a bikini pic, too," I added as Nikki and Dr. Radisha looked me up and down.

"Oh, you *want* to show it," Dr. Radisha said.

"Yeah, I had two kids," I said confidently and reasoned that I would feel a sense of freedom.

"I can't because I don't want our patients to see the pictures…"

"And spend a whole session talking about it," she added.

Nikki admitted that she still gets self-conscious, especially seeing BBL (referring to a voluptuous backside).

"Girl, have you seen yourself in "It's Not Fair (music video where she is in a bikini throughout)?" I turned to her in disbelief. Everyone laughed.

Cancel the Filter

* * *

Ben Baller was standing in the doorway on his way to do his individual interview when I mentioned, "If my husband could carry the baby, I would have a third."

"Don't have three. It's a mistake," he said.

"Wait, why are three bad?" I asked.

"It's not bad, it's just that you're outnumbered," he said, matter-of-factly.

* * *

As I rushed upstairs, Nikki had her purse over her shoulder, heading out. I surprised myself and said, "Oh, Nikki. Before you go, can I take a picture? Sorry, totally fangirling here."

Nikki squatted her approximately five-feet-five-inch frame down to my five feet-two inches and we had one of my pictures for Instagram. I felt like a weirdo and that much braver.

The day ended on an even sweeter note, taking my husband to a French restaurant in the city. He polished off a spicy lamb sausage and brie panini, and I had the duck confit with au gratin potatoes. He deserved a great meal for all his support. He told me he was proud of me for speaking on the panel, and I later discovered that he recorded my clips on stage.

* * *

The day after the panel, I was tagged in a video by Miss Asia 2020, a woman who disclosed to the audience that she lost a friend to suicide. She noted that she did not feel up to coming to the summit but was encouraged by her friend Drex Lee, a famed videographer. She expressed her gratitude for the information she internalized. One of the most rewarding aspects of the summit and the work that we did was the opportunity to have a positive impact on someone's life. I am so grateful that she experienced some sense of support and healing.

Cancel the Filter on AAPI Representation & Diversity, Equity, and Inclusion

While many celebrities, colleagues, and I have been fortunate to be invited to speak on behalf of the mental health and AAPI communities, it is important to acknowledge that we could never speak for everyone in these communities or all Asian American and Pacific Islanders. The term Asian American is also an umbrella term that does not accurately depict the diversity among and within Asian ethnic groups. There is also an emotional tax that is placed on many under-represented individuals to be educators of race, culture, and ethnicity because the onerous is placed on them instead of the learner. Therefore, when I am in the community at various events and talks, and even throughout this book, I emphasize that I am speaking from *my* perspective and experiences and welcome others' differing experiences. Of course, I'd prefer a cordial conversation. Through my participation, my intentions are to start and contribute to important conversations in many settings, among children, peers, and colleagues, and build community.

Guest Speaker at my Daughter's School for Asian American, Pacific Islander Heritage & Mental Health Awareness Month

One of my greatest honors to date is being invited by Oz's third-grade teacher to speak in front of two classes for Asian American Pacific Islander Heritage and Mental Health Awareness Month. I surprised Oz because the teacher did not tell her that I was coming to the class, and I joined the virtual meeting during class time. She was screaming and

Cancel the Filter

tearing up. Her facial expressions of surprise, glee, and pride are something I can't describe because they made me feel like I did something "right" as a parent. I'm going to ride the "cool mom" wave and save the video clip my husband recorded. I'll play it for her when she is a teenager and she may not have that same expression if I show up at her school.

It was great to discuss the importance of mental health with the students, and how learning coping skills early on in life could be beneficial throughout one's life. I asked students what they do to cope with stress. One student said, "When my mom is stressed, she does Retail Therapy."

I had my therapist face on, and because I am friends with the mom, stated, "Your mom is a very fashionable person!"

One student asked, "Is Thai, Asian? My mom felt sad leaving Thailand." This student seemed to want and need mentorship. She also said, "I only have four YouTube subscribers."

"Don't focus on the numbers, which is hard to do, but continue to do work you love and are proud of."

My husband threw those words back at me when I told him that my social media numbers dropped. In his kind bluntness, "Didn't you say to that kid not to worry about numbers?

Touché.

It was also a wonderful opportunity to discuss the role of a psychologist and how podcasting is a way to provide help to people through storytelling. The class's demographics are very diverse and broadening their career choices will also hopefully inspire them to learn many things. Additionally, it also helps that Oz's teacher is a mental health and diversity advocate. In fact, during a parent-teacher conference, I asked her if she knew of any children's books written by Asian American authors that our daughter could read.

To our surprise, she said, "I have one right here."

She later sent Oz home with several books by Asian American authors for our daughter's reading list. She also sent me a list of eleven books by Asian American authors for adults to read. It is so powerful to see a teacher who champions diversity and truly values it.

There is a reason why she was Oz's favorite elementary school teacher and Educator of the Year in 2023.

Stephanie J. Wong

Representation in Hollywood

Making History: Shang-Chi and the Legend of the Ten Rings

With the kids returning to school, and the buzz surrounding the Asian-actor-led Marvel movie, *Shang-Chi and the Legend of the Ten Rings*, we decided to rent out a theater for a private screening. We got thirty of our friends together. There was so much excitement, and all the families took pictures next to the movie's posters. It was the first time I'd seen *all* of us take pictures, not just me for my Instagram. There was something different about seeing our faces reflected in the characters.

Have you ever gone to a movie where most audience members are under ten years of age? Well, *you are in for a treat*. The kids sat in the front together because that was the only area where adults weren't sitting. I swear I could hear Oz talking throughout the movie, which she got from her father. At one point, my youngest had to go to the bathroom and annoyingly, I had to go as well. She was also running up and down the aisles when she wanted more snacks.

I invited my friend from work and her brother, and I was worried that they were not having an enjoyable time because of all the chatter. Fortunately, her brother had already seen the movie the night before. Then the kid behind us began to read the subtitles aloud, which was hilarious and a bit annoying. I gave her the benefit of the doubt that it was because her brother couldn't read. The most heart-warming point of the movie was when the main character's mother appeared in a Cheongsam, a traditional Chinese dress, and the kid gasped, "She's so beautiful." This moment captured what representation truly means to me.

When we returned home, we all agreed that we wanted to rewatch it on Disney, but it was not yet available. I was so glad that I anticipated wanting the toys from the movie and purchased the toys prior to watching the movie. We watched YouTube clip after clip of the cast, and I admired how Simu Liu, the main actor continued to be unapologetically Asian, drinking boba, serving 85 Degrees C Bakery sweets at the premiere, and bringing all the Asian creators he had

Cancel the Filter

befriended over the years to events. I couldn't be prouder to be Asian American.

* * *

The Kids Experience Being Starstruck!

Simu Liu launched a book tour for his autobiography, *We Are Dreamers*, and I jumped on buying tickets for one of the book signing events. Our kids watched Shang-Chi more times than I can count, and I credit the movie for continuing to facilitate pride in being Asian American. I also absolutely love book tours. I enjoyed a birthday outing during Ali Wong's book tour with a friend.

The event was postponed due to him filming the *Barbie* movie, so we had a month between the purchase and the actual event. In the month leading up to the event, the kids asked me, "Mommy, can you get him on the podcast?"

"I would love to, but I don't think I can. You can ask him though."

I made business cards for the event and was quite proud of myself for figuring out how to generate a QR code to put on the card. The kids came up with questions they wanted to ask him, and wrote warm notes on index cards, attaching the business cards as well. The questions went out the window when it was our turn to meet him. Simu smiled warmly at Ya Ya, and she immediately said, "Would you be on my mommy's podcast?"

His face scrunched up, and he replied, "I don't know your mommy's podcast, but I could...may...be check it out...You are well-trained."

I felt my face begin to heat up.

"They are employed!" my husband chuckled, and I parroted this.

I put my hands up, and said, "I didn't do this."

"I don't believe you," he said.

My face burnt up some more.

Ya Ya asked if she could have a picture with her Polaroid camera.

"One camera per group," said the attendant.

We purchased four books. Note to self: Split up during book signings.

For our pictures, Ya Ya was staring at him. I later asked her what she was thinking and feeling.

"My heart was beating 2,000 times, and I was trying to figure out if he was real or a spy?"

Ya Ya has watched too many Marvel movies and shows.

Oz was so nervous that she didn't ask her question, "Is Chloe Bennet [actress from Agents of S.H.I.E.L.D] cool?" despite me assuring her, "I'm sure she is."

She also wanted to ask him about his role in the *Barbie* movie, but anxiety prevented her from doing so. Instead, she said it softly to my husband who rarely feels shame. "She wants to know if the Barbie movie will be family-friendly?" he asked.

"Uhhh. It will be PG-13 so you can decide," Simu said, making eye contact with me. I nervously chuckled.

I felt more embarrassed during the interaction than starstruck or joyful because while I obviously would have enjoyed having him on the show, the kids were the ones who really wanted him to be a guest. For me, the only celebrities I would repeatedly, shamelessly, and unapologetically ask to be on the show are BTS members because they have had an indelible impact on my life.

Later, Oz said, "I hope he comes on the podcast because it was weird asking him!" *She has a high EQ/emotional quotient.*

While he told staff to hold onto the cards, at publishing, we unfortunately never heard from him.

Bringing Home the Gold

It was a rare moment of silence in our house, as three generations of Asian American females listened to Chloé Zhao's speech at the Academy Awards. It was not lost on me that my daughters were seeing someone who was Chinese American like them, accept one of the highest honors in film and entertainment. What resonated with me the most was the characters from the poem she and her father would read and remember together, which translated to, "People are born inherently good at birth." She urged people to find the good in people as she has among people around the world, even though it can be difficult at times. It was the speech that Asian Americans everywhere needed to hear after so many traumatic hate crimes were reported during the pandemic.

In 2023, Michelle Yeoh, a long-time, global role model in the Asian and AAPI community was awarded both the Golden Globe and the Oscar for the movie, *Everything Everywhere All at Once*. Her co-star, Ke Huy Quan, a childhood actor from blockbuster hits such as *Indiana Jones and the Temple of Doom* and *The Goonies*, also won both the Golden Globe and Oscar for his role. While the awards do not negate the history of Asian stereotypes depicted in Hollywood—buck-toothed, yellow face, slanty eyes, and bad accents—it made a statement that our contributions are valid and that we have a lot to offer in entertainment.

To Be Martha Washington or Not to Be Martha Washington? That was the question in Fifth Grade.

Despite the diversity and inclusion "movement" that was occurring in Hollywood, Oz's fifth-grade class was still being asked to participate in the colonial project, and Oz was asked to present as Martha Washington. Students would also receive bonus points for dressing up like their assigned person in history. The script was innocuous enough, seemingly excerpted from Martha's Wikipedia page, such as helping soldiers during the war by sewing. The instructions for the outfit were to "Dress as a colonial woman, carrying a pair of socks."

As an elementary student, I was not taught the complex history of our nation. In middle school, I was fortunate to have diverse teachers who included a curriculum on slavery. For example, in eighth grade, my class watched *Roots*, and in high school, I was assigned to read, *A People's History of the United States*, which discussed the horrific acts that were committed against Native Americans for colonialists to obtain their land. From that point on, I have learned that most individuals and cultural histories are not taught and are therefore invisible in the teachings of American history. Therefore, I was not particularly thrilled that our Asian American daughter would be dressing up as a colonial White woman. While it seems that Martha had many great traits, she and George were also slave owners on large plantations.

I communicated my concerns to my family. While my husband said he agreed with me, he also did not want our daughter to be ostracized, canceled, or adversely impact her group's grade. Initially, I did not contact her teacher who notably is also Asian American. However, when I presented at a company about AAPI mental health, emphasizing the need for an inclusive work environment, I told the employees about our situation. One person's comment changed my mind about contacting the teacher. They said, "In many parts of the country, that would be wrong."

I gathered my courage to contact the teacher, despite my family looking at me quizzically. I wrote:

Hi TEACHER,

Hope all is well! I've gone back and forth about sending this email, but I am hoping to stay true to my values as an AAPI advocate. My husband and I do not want Oz's feelings or grade to be compromised as I understand it is a group effort. I feel very uncomfortable that Oz and her classmates have to dress up as colonialists, particularly since there was widespread oppression due to colonialists. While the script about Martha Washington seems innocuous, it does not include the full context of her life—being a slave and plantation owner. It appears from reports that she had many wonderful qualities, but I'm not sure if dressing up like her is consistent with diversity principles.

Last year, I asked TEACHER B if Asian American history would be incorporated into the curriculum, and unfortunately, it was not. Asian American Heritage Month is in May, and it would be a great opportunity to have the curriculum incorporated. TEACHER C was fantastic and gave Oz quite a few books by Asian American authors. I understand that the district has curriculum requirements, but sharing various cultures' histories would be very inclusive and embrace diverse students' heritage.

Please let us know what could be an alternative to fulfill the assignment and not jeopardize the group's grade. Thank you for listening!

Cancel the Filter

The teacher immediately responded and cc'd the principal:

Good evening,
    Thank you for sharing your insights and values. I appreciate it and will take it into consideration moving forward.
    If Oz would like, as an alternative assignment, she can pick an Asian American figure in history to research and present to the class, as this is both a history and a public speaking assignment. The blurb about her person can be four to five sentences stating their background and significance in history. If she would like to dress the part, that would be fantastic!
    Oz already mentioned that you would be away during the day of our presentation due to a previously scheduled vacation, so her group has her part covered and will not be penalized for the decision not to participate.
    Thank you again for sharing your thoughts and insights,
    TEACHER.

Following the response, my husband said that it's up to Oz what she would like to do. I was flabbergasted! Did I just go through all that trouble to have her still dress up as a colonialist? I began researching prominent Asian American historical figures, and we decided on Joyce Chen who introduced northern Chinese cuisine to American palates, in addition to the Chinese buffet concept. She owned Joyce Chen Restaurant, authored her own cookbook, and had her own cooking show on PBS, "Joyce Chen Cooks." I told Oz that she may not understand fully what I'm trying to teach her, but she will later. She saw that it was very important to me, and she agreed to present on Joyce Chen. Oz wore an apron and my jade necklace. We also had an image of Joyce's cookbook taped on the cover of another book. In the end, I was happy to stand up for what was right, but it was again very uncomfortable and daunting. However, hopefully, it will facilitate discussion about ways to incorporate Asian American history into classrooms.

Stephanie J. Wong

Open House or the Asian American, Native Hawaiian, and Pacific Islander (AANHPI) Heritage White House Event?

To honor AANHPI history, the White House hosts an annual event. In 2023, I was invited by a friend to attend the AANHPI White House Event, which led me to scramble to find a flight to Washington DC that would enable me to attend the event the day after arrival. I would then have to return home the day after the event so I could attend the girls' open house at school. As I continued to debate whether to go or not, thinking I would miss out on an opportunity, my best friend looked up the ticket to the events and told me they were free to the public.

Despite addressing the misperception that this was an exclusive, invite-only event, I still had FOMO, particularly since a friend was chosen by Madame VP herself, Kamala Harris, to co-interview her. However, I was clear in my priority: My family. I will not compromise attending these school events because these are literally once-in-a-lifetime. You cannot go back to when Oz and Ya Ya are in fifth and third grade, respectively. I recalled my third grade open house, showing my parents my diorama, and how much that meant to me. I also reasoned, maybe a few people will remember I was at the event, but my children will remember me being there for them. My close friend also disclosed that her friend passed away at thirty-nine years old to cancer. That hit me. When people look back on their lives, they don't focus on the awards or prestige, but on their loved ones, and how much love they mutually gave each other. I would pick the open house over the White House any day.

My Sanity

While self-care has become a buzzword in the past several years, I firmly believe that everyone needs healthy coping skills and ways to facilitate joy, relaxation, and in moderation, escapism. I've noticed that as Oz and Ya Ya grow up, there is less of an emphasis on play in all aspects of their lives. There isn't any less of a need as we age to have recreation and leisure, but daily life makes it challenging to incorporate these activities. For me, it really takes an ongoing, conscious effort to prioritize taking care of myself. One of the major ways that I do so is by being a member of the global superstars Bangtan Seonyondan aka Bulletproof Boy Scouts aka Behind-the-Scene (BTS) fandom, Adorable Representative M.C. for Youth (ARMY).

For those who haven't been a part of a fandom, I'll try to describe what a profound impact it can have on one's life. BTS debuted as a seven-member group in 2013 in Korea under Big Hit Entertainment and were viewed as an underdog because they were not being managed by a major Korean entertainment company. Let me paint a picture of their struggles. All seven members, Kim Namjoon aka RM, Kim Seokjin aka Jin, Min Yoongi aka Suga, Jeon Hoseok aka j-hope, Park Jimin, Kim Taehyung aka V, and Jeon Jungkook, slept in one room in bunk beds, practiced in a park near their apartment because the practice room was so small they could touch the ceilings. They survived on very little food and money with one member delivering food in between twelve to fifteen hours of practice a day. With their hard work, group chemistry, each member's unique charms and personality, and the support of ARMY, BTS broke into the American music market that no other K-pop group had ever been able to. Therefore, ARMY consider them to have had an American debut in 2017 when they performed at the Billboard Music Awards.

Stephanie J. Wong

I became an ARMY when they made their American debut. From there, I took a deep dive into their discography, which included songs about societal expectations of going to school, getting good grades and securing a "good" job. As Suga says, "It's okay not to have a dream." By looking at ARMY's translations of the Korean lyrics to English, predating YouTube subtitles, I learned BTS also addresses mental health, loving yourself, and mutual love between BTS and ARMY. BTS's generosity and message of love and acceptance led ARMY to be generous. For example, when BTS donated $1 million to Black Lives Matter, ARMY matched the donation.

Being an ARMY has led me to:

- Meet other ARMY from all around the world, virtually and in- person.
- Continue studying Korean for over seven years so that I could begin to understand lyrics and interviews. (This has been a very difficult feat to learn a language in adulthood.)
- Have an outlet to smile and relieve stress.
- Travel for concerts.
- Not feel afraid to work seven days a week if I like what I am doing.

So in 2018, BTS announced their tour dates and they were going to perform in concert in the Bay Area. Clearly because they are my favorite group of all time, I was willing to pay a pretty penny for the tickets. Well, guess what? So was everyone else.

I enlisted the help of my co-worker, brother, and husband to help me get tickets. My husband got the closest, but on the purchase screen, a message appeared that someone else had bought the tickets. Therefore, none of us could get tickets at face value. We learned the ticket site holds back tickets and sells them at four times face value. It seems ridiculous, but I purchased four tickets at $800 each for my kids, husband, and me. I felt instant relief that I was going to this historic concert!

My husband, forever the entrepreneur, jokingly posted the tickets for re-sale at $2,500 a ticket. After a few weeks, he called me on speaker

Cancel the Filter

phone with his co-worker and excitedly said, "Someone bought the tickets!"

"So, you're saying that we don't have tickets?" I felt tears start to brim in my eyes.

"I thought you'd be happy," he said.

I began to cry, and his co-worker directed him to take me off speaker.

My husband explained that there were other tickets. We almost instantly purchased tickets for $1,000 a seat. Therefore, we technically attended the concert for free and made extra money, which we put towards buying a house. So, BTS technically helped us buy a house. Please, ARMY, I love you. Don't hate me.

When the day of the concert arrived, we rushed to get into the concert venue. Lines had already formed to enter the fan area just to get a postcard. There were ARMY everywhere, dancing and singing to BTS songs. Oz was cranky. To be fair, my kids were the youngest humans at the concert, and people did the, "They are so cute with their BTS [cartoon character] shirts." To appease the kids, we all went to the restroom and then got them Dippin' Dots before finding our seats. The stadium began to fill in and the ARMY was singing along to BTS music videos on the jumbo screen.

The lights went out and the crowd roared! My youngest was two feet tall. After an hour, the girls felt tired, and fell asleep! Yes, at a larger-than-life concert with screaming ARMY everywhere, they fell asleep. This dates back to when my husband and I were raising them as infants. We lived at my in-laws' house, and they spoke very loudly, which is where my husband gets it from. Therefore, the kids are accustomed to sleeping through noise. My husband recorded one of BTS' biggest hits for the girls, which they would watch later. People may judge us for buying expensive tickets for toddlers, but we did not have babysitters that night, and they also love BTS. Plus, essentially, they were free with the ticket situation. There are some concerts and events that I will leave them out of, but this was not one of them.

Pro tip: A nap before a concert is a necessity even if it is during the ride from school to the concert.

While I no longer have to compete for professional internships or jobs, I now have to enter the Hunger Games for every BTS ticket sale. So when I have them in my e-wallet, I covet them. As the pandemic took so much out of everyone around the globe, I continued my seven-day a week grind and looked forward to eventually using my fifth-row tickets to BTS' Map of the Soul (MOTS) tour. The concert had already been postponed once, but I took comfort in knowing that I could keep my tickets. As the pandemic raged on, HYBE, previously known as Big Hit Entertainment, eventually canceled the concert. I was devastated. This was the one event, the thing that gave me hope and pushed me to keep on providing care to patients on my caseload. I was burnt out but seemed to have relatively stable mental health. I am not embarrassed to admit that I cried. My husband even recorded me for his Tik Tok, crying under a blanket (sure, look it up).

Shortly after, South Korean, President Moon Jae-In appointed the members of BTS as presidential envoys, which is one of the highest honors. They would travel with him to the US for the UN Summit to discuss global initiatives. As expected, their appearance garnered millions of views and positive attention to these initiatives. They informed the world that they were vaccinated and encouraged everyone to do so. They performed "Permission to Dance" in the wee hours of the night, and made a speech, this time with all seven members speaking. I was so proud of them.

A few days later, they announced four shows in Southern California for their Permission to Dance on Stage tour! The ticketing company sent out an announcement that MOTS ticket holders would be first for the pre-sale of the tickets with VIP ticket holders going first. I was so relieved that I would have first dibs. However, I discovered that they did not send me the code. I then tried contacting the company, which eventually informed me that I would then receive automated emails that would get sent to a customer service team. I eventually got my code!

Well, then came the shitshow. On the second day, my husband and I entered the waiting room early as VIP holders did the day before. My husband did research via Twitter and YouTube to see how the ticketing

Cancel the Filter

went the previous day. Since so many people entered early, the ticketing company released a statement that the waiting room would open thirty minutes early. Yet when I tried to enter, I received the message, "Account is not linked." I was frantic at this point, and Twitter was going off that many people had this issue. I eventually got in after fifteen minutes but by that time, I was late in the queue. I was able to score 200-level tickets and was disappointed because they were still very far from the stage—no soundcheck, no floor, not even 100-level. My husband reassured me that we could resell the tickets and purchase the ones I wanted. Later, I discovered that most people got 400- or 500-level tickets so I should feel fortunate, but somehow, I felt robbed. I had to try again the next day for the ARMY pre-sale.

The night before the ARMY pre-sale, I did not receive a code. There was confusion about Weverse, HYBE's platform, and whether we should have registered there and with the ticketing company. I tried to contact the company again, but it was the same process. They responded with my same code and when I tried to log on, my account wasn't linked again. Panic settled before I tried to tweet and email to resolve this so I could get in. That day, they even released way more tickets because the previous day went so poorly. I missed out on that opportunity. Same with the day after that for verified fans.

Ultimately, someone bought our tickets, which were priced similarly to others. However, we likely could have gotten more. We made a hasty purchase on another ticketing site, which told us that our tickets were general admission, but those didn't exist. Reviews for this site were not good at all, with many saying that they were cheated out of their money. We had paid thousands for what we thought were floor tickets. Constant emailing to the company led to automated emails.

I then decided to take my despair to where else? Social media. I DM'd the CEO of the ticketing platform on both Twitter and Instagram. I later tweeted my appeal that I worked seven days a week with the hope that I would be able to use my tickets. In a few days, I received an email asking me which day I wanted to purchase tickets for, and that I would receive a special link to request them. I wanted to believe this was real. I DM'd the CEO again to ask if this was legit. He said it was and that he wanted to help. I also added the other company to this tweet who assured me that they would assist me. The latter company continued to send me automated emails. I then submitted my request for floor tickets and paid the money. I was awaiting the tickets in my account before proceeding to request a refund from the latter company. What a mess!

Finally, the impossible happened. The latter company refunded the full amount! But the more amazing thing happened later, I received the special link from the CEO's team and requested the best tickets possible. A ticket agent was assigned to me and shortly after my seventeen-year-old fur baby passed, I received Section A1, Row 30 tickets! My fur son was looking out for us, and I was so grateful!

My First "Break-Up"

Since I married my high school sweetheart, I have fortunately not had to face the devastation of multiple heartbreaks. So, when BTS announced they were taking a hiatus as a group to pursue solo endeavors, I had to take a day to fully process my feelings. Who am I kidding? It took me way more than a day to process my feelings. While Suga made it clear, "It's not like we're disbanding. We are just living separately for a while."

I empathized with them about working non-stop, industry expectations, and meeting ARMY for concerts and through virtual channels. I respected them needing time individually to explore their identities so they could come back stronger. I had to rely on their sincerity as most groups would not be as raw with their emotions. I was also grateful that they gave us more music during the pandemic, particularly since they didn't plan to do so. They planned to announce the hiatus after the song, "ON " was released in 2020. While I empathize, I can't avoid the loss, the void I feel. When you are connected to a global community, it is hard to imagine that core not being there, but as BTS says, "The Best is Yet to Come."

I was sitting on the outer edges of our bathtub in Cabo watching the FESTA dinner, crying with them. My husband kept coming in and checking on my reactions every ten minutes or so. When I finally came

Cancel the Filter

out of the bathroom, the kids we were vacationing with, said, "Stephanie looks emo. She is wearing black and has a messy bun." Note: I looked like this before I watched the video. I moped the whole day, irritable that they wouldn't be together for a while.

There were so many reminders— bags, sanitizers, magazines, and concert gear. I just didn't imagine that Vegas would be the last concert before a long break. I don't have regrets, although it would've been nice to have gone to the second day of the concert in Los Angeles, particularly since the crowd was included in "For Youth." Also, I could've had tickets for the second day of the concert in Vegas—floor seats! Regardless, it has been a great five years for me. What's more, I felt heartbroken that they feared for their fans.

But soon enough, they released loads of content, which they filmed in anticipation of the hiatus. Jungkook and Charlie Puth released "Left and Right," and the vocal line released a song with Benny Blanco and Snoop Dog. j-hope headlined Lollapalooza. Each member released a vlog.

I listen and watch their "For Youth " performance every day and it calms me. Whenever I drive, I have "Proof" on. Although it felt like my first break-up, it really was not because they are still showing us their talents! All the members have released solo projects, including Jin releasing a single with Coldplay, j-hope releasing Jack in the Box, RM collaborating with Anderson Paak, Jimin showing his swag on "Set Me Free," Jungkook even breaking BTS' records of consecutive weeks on the Billboard Global 200 chart, V showcasing his deep voice, and Suga going on tour.

Did I Drink a Cup of Tea with Suga? Two Psychologists Engaging in Self-Care with Agust D

Another round of the *Hunger Games* was announced in the spring of 2023 when the second eldest BTS member, Suga announced a solo tour, with a stop in the Bay Area. Of course, there was the standard, complicated process of registering as an official ARMY member on Weverse and then registering on Ticketmaster for an ARMY presale code to purchase the tickets. I ensured I had followed the instructions down to the letter. But even with the registration, you were not guaranteed to receive a code the night before the sale, and of course, I did not. I began monitoring the ridiculously priced tickets immediately after the presale. My computer and Capital One cash back extension tracked my monitoring and offered me cash back if I bought the tickets via StubHub. The offer kept increasing every day via email, and I decided to purchase VIP general admission tickets as I would receive 24% cashback. I ended up paying less than face value for these tickets!

While my husband would attend the concert with me, he was more than happy for me to offer my friend the ticket. I met this friend at a conference, and we immediately bonded over our love for BTS after she noticed my watch's wristband. Now two BTS ARMY psychologists were planning on having the best time! She planned her trip from Hawaii to the Bay Area and even bought tickets to go with her son the night before our concert day.

After weeks of planning, my friend arrived, and I contacted VIP Live Nation to inquire about the VIP event timeline. The representative noted that these amenities were not transferable from fan to fan, and the only workaround was for the original ticket holder to add my name to the alternate will-call pick-up. This non-transferrable situation is ridiculous because everyone knows people sell these amenities. Also, after doing recon on the VIP amenities, fans were expected to line up to receive their numbered VIP wristbands, which dictated the order in which they entered early to the merch and sound check. While the tickets indicated "no camping allowed," people in other cities were camping in areas with high crime rates.

I immediately contacted StubHub about the situation, and they agreed to contact the seller and resolve the issue in a few hours. After several hours passed, I contacted them an hour after the estimated time. They agreed to contact the seller again and contact me in a few hours, but there was still no response so my husband called back that night and the next day. By the time my friend and her son left for their concert, we were battling on the phone with a manager. The initial representative offered three options: 1) Twenty-five-percent refund; 2) Comparable

Cancel the Filter

seats, which would require canceling our current order and receiving a link to choose between the proposed seats; 3) A full refund. But when the manager came on the phone, she said we only had one—the first. The rationale was that we still had our tickets, we just couldn't use the amenities to which my husband replied, "What's the point of VIP tickets without the VIP activities?"

Since we had no other option, we took the twenty-five-percent refund. But he called back to describe his displeasure at the way the situation was being handled. My husband is extremely nice, but when I cry, he becomes assertive. This manager was more empathic and suggested we go to the venue and assess the situation. Our tickets were labeled GA Section B, which we knew did not exist because it was standing-room only. VIP Live Nation also confirmed that if the seller did not add me as an alternate pick-up, they could theoretically still use the amenities.

The day of the concert arrived with no VIP activities to go to, and we decided to sell our general admission tickets at a price that would enable us to purchase better tickets. Since my friend went to the concert, she had intel as to which seats would give us a close-up view of this idol. Luckily, someone purchased the tickets with the full understanding that they were not VIP, and we ended up in Section 128, Row 3! We were so close that we saw his porcelain skin! While it is a shame that there is a conglomerate that holds all the power in distributing tickets, this situation turned out better than we could have imagined thanks to my husband.

Love and Canceling the Filter

As I was finishing the edits on this book, my dear friend and colleague, Priscilla Azcueta finished a long, hard battle with multiple cancers. Even throughout this multi-year battle, Priscilla maintained her enthusiasm, warmth, and giving nature. After she received the news that despite her will to live, there were no other medical treatments for the cancers, she tearfully said, "But you know what? I've received a lot of love, and I've given *so* much love!"

Priscilla was someone who fully understood the meaning of life–love. Love does not equate to the absence of conflict or hurt, but rather, can you come back from conflict? Can you clear up misunderstandings and conflict, take ownership for what you contributed to the conflict, and genuinely apologize? As most of us know, this is no easy feat and of course, there are relationships that are physically, emotionally, and psychologically unsafe to be in or engage in. Love is setting boundaries and mutually supporting each other through good times and hardships. It is about building bonds one-on-one and in groups and communities.

Love starts with me, reflecting on myself and fostering gratitude. I continue to take an honest, unfiltered assessment of how I feel about myself and how I live, think, interact with, and treat others. How much am I taking care of myself? Am I living consistently with my values? Am I giving love and being mindful that I'm more prone to give love and support than ask for it in return? My answers vary depending on when I'm answering the questions, but I now know that love means canceling the filter on acting the way I think other people want me to be.

Continuing to cancel the filter means aspiring to be a kind, generous person even though I know I have flaws and imperfections. When I ask people who tend to be hard on themselves, "Who is perfect?" The majority answer, "No one." I had one person answer, "God." Either

Cancel the Filter

way, it makes life harder when we hold ourselves to unrealistic expectations.

So join me in canceling the filter on how we present the way we live our lives. Live authentically. Share your stories, struggles, and wins with others. Speak up when something feels unjust or unfairly and severely critical. As someone who feels behind on work, household, and childcare tasks, I attest that this is normal. A chaotic lifestyle is a norm for many working mothers. It is in our shared struggle that we foster empathy, gratitude, and love.

Gratitude

This book is dedicated to my co-authors, my children, husband, family, and friends who are helping me write the story of my life.

To my husband who has always let me get more sleep than him, teaching our kids at a young age to, "Let Mommy sleep." You are one of the most selfless people I know, supporting me in jumping into multiple projects at once. Challenging gender roles has been one of the ways you have canceled the filter, and taught our daughters that they have a voice and can use it. You have been the love of my life since high school and I am fortunate we have chosen each other to go on this journey together.

To Oz, you have a pure heart just like your father, your kindness draws people to you. You are an amazing baker and are full of grit and determination. You don't back down when something is challenging!

To Ya Ya, your wit, humor, and emotional intelligence continue to amaze me. You are quick to learn new things and bring others so much joy. You are creative and always thinking of new games or art projects.

To my parents, thank you for giving birth to my sibling and me. It hasn't always been easy, but we are close because we have faced challenging times. You are amazing grandparents and the girls are growing up well because of your love and support.

To my brother who is the only person who knows what it was like during our childhood. I'm so glad we can always laugh together. Gobble, Gobble!

To my in-laws who raised a selfless, generous, and humorous man. You have always helped us in our times of need.

To my working parents out there and my readers, thank you for your support. Know that you are not alone and I'm right here along with you! Please connect and share your stories with me through my social media pages! Clearly, I also love a funny story!

Author's Notes

Here are a few pop culture references that may be new to you:

Blood, Sweat, and Tears is a hit song by BTS that talks about growth in the face of temptation.

Cardi B. is the stage name of Belcalis Marlenis Almánzar Cephus, an American rapper who is also famous for her charismatic personality. She went viral during the pandemic for the way she said, "Corona Virus."

Emily in Paris is a series starring Lily Collins as Emily, an American who moves to Paris for a job at a marketing firm. Her transition to living in Paris is not an easy one.

Agents of S.H.I.E.L.D. (Strategic Homeland Intervention, Enforcement, and Logistics Division), is a Marvel series following government spies who attempt to maintain peace in a world filled with individuals with superpowers. **Enoch** serves as an anthropologist of an alien species, Chronicoms, and helps the agents save the world many times over. **Chloe Bennet** plays Daisy Johnson/Quake who has the power of creating the effects of earthquakes.

Fast & the Furious is a movie franchise characterized by action, high-speed driving, family, squad goals, and confusion about who is good and bad.

FESTA is an annual event celebrating BTS' Korean debut with ARMY.

Hunger Games is a dystopian trilogy written by Suzanne Collins where

Author's Notes

two children from each of twelve districts are selected to battle to the death. The books were adapted for the big screen.

Poopsie Slime Surprise is a doll that comes with various slime surprises, including a purse that can hold slime. This is every parent's dream.

Rosanna Pansino is a content creator known for her baking videos on her YouTube channel, Nerdy Nummies. She is also an author, actress, judge, and singer.

Twilight is a saga written by Stephenie Meyer where the human protagonist, Bella Swan experiences the complications of falling in love with a vampire. The books were adapted for the big screen.

About the Author

Stephanie J. Wong, Ph.D. is an Asian American, licensed clinical psychologist, entrepreneur, BTS ARMY, and founder and host of the award winning, Color of Success Podcast, which seeks to destigmatize mental health among Asian Americans/Canadians and ethnic minorities. She works in private practice with Tech professionals, most of which are ethnic minorities, and at a hospital, serving military veterans. Dr. Wong was recently lauded as one of Asian Hustle Network's 50 Unsung Heroes. Her training in clinical interviewing has led to fireside chats with diverse podcast guests about advancing their careers and addressing mental health and cultural identity. Notable guests have included celebrities, Margaret Cho, stars of Bling Empire, Andrew Phung of Kim's Convenience, content creator, Jessica Woo, the Cast of Netflix's Partner Track, and more.

Dr. Wong is a keynote speaker in academic, entertainment, and corporate settings, sharing her expertise in Asian American mental health, diversity, equity, and inclusion (DE&I), working with underrepresented populations, and empowering Women of Color. She also discusses the treatment of anxiety, depression, substance use, work related stress, and relationship and cultural concerns.

To learn more about Dr. Wong, visit drstephaniejwong.com

To join the Color of Success family and dive into content, visit colorofsuccesspodcast.com.

Join on Social Media:

Instagram: @color_of_success
Linkedin: @stephaniewong2
YouTube: @colorofsuccess
Facebook: @colorofsuccess
TikTok: @colorofsuccesspodcast
X (formerly Twitter): @DrStephJWong

www.ingramcontent.com/pod-product-compliance
Lightning Source LLC
LaVergne TN
LVHW021047100526
838202LV00079B/4708